Religion at the Crossroads

Byzantium

The Turks

The Rise and Fall of Empires

Religion at the Crossroads

Byzantium

The Turks

Joyce Milton
Byzantium

Rafael Steinberg
Sarah Lewis
The Turks

Preface by Ron William Walden
Department of Religious Studies
Bethany College

CASSELL
LONDON

CASSELL LTD.
35 Red Lion Square, London WC1R 4SG
and at Sydney, Auckland, Toronto, Johannesburg,
an affiliate of
Macmillan Publishing Co., Inc.,
New York.

© Rizzoli Editore 1980

First published in Great Britain 1980

ISBN 0 304 30575 8

Printed in Italy

Authors: Joyce Milton, Rafael Steinberg, and Sarah Lewis
Picture Researcher, Janet Adams
Assistant Picture Researcher, Noreen O'Gara

Consultants
    Byzantium: Ron William Walden
    The Turks: Mark Heller

Design Implementation, Designworks

Rizzoli Editore

Authors of the Italian Edition
    Introduction: Professor Ovidio Dallera
    Byzantium: Professor Andrea Guiducci
    The Turks: Dr. Italo Sordi
    Maps: Fernando Russo
Idea and Realization, Harry C. Lindinger
Graphic Design, Gerry Valsecchi
General Editorial Supervisor, Ovidio Dallera

Contents

Preface

The two civilizations—Byzantine and Turkish—that played out their rivalry across the Aegean as the Middle Ages waned have always proved enigmatic to Western Europeans. Cosmopolitan, exotic Byzantium has exercised a perennial fascination on the imagination of the West and yet has stubbornly eluded understanding. The Turkish Empire has emerged as the West's foremost caricature of the cruel and alien state, menacing and at the same time alluring in its violence and sensuousness.

The Western misunderstanding of Byzantine civilization began in late classical times, when the Roman Empire began its long decline. The populous eastern provinces had never been thoroughly Latinized, and as trade and travel decreased, the two civilizations of the Roman Empire developed separately—each an heir of Rome, each a champion of Christ, each a stranger to the other. The persistent religious disputes between Byzantines and Latins provide the clearest evidence of this alienation. Later, as the intellectual center of gravity shifted from the Mediterranean region to northern Europe, an even greater spiritual distance intervened between Western thinkers and the "schismatical Greeks."

Western attitudes toward Greek politics and society have typically been marked by condescension. Occidentals saw themselves as simple, vigorous, and straightforward and regarded imperial Constantinople as effete and overcivilized. Ceaseless palace intrigue and rule by eunuchs and women loomed large in European views of Byzantine statecraft. Yet the West's sneering sense of superiority often served to mask admiration and envy for the city on the Golden Horn. A great French chronicler of the Fourth Crusade has nothing but scorn for Byzantine politics and recounts the sack of Constantinople by the crusaders in 1204 in an almost matter-of-fact way. Yet when describing the spoils, he cannot resist hyperbole:

> The booty gained was so great that none could tell you the end of it: gold and silver, and vessels and precious stones, and samite, and cloth of silk, and robes vair and grey, and ermine, and every choicest thing found upon the earth. And well does Geoffry of Villehardouin, the Marshal of Champagne, bear witness, that never, since the world was created, had so much booty been won in any city.

Such wide-eyed wonder at Constantinople's wealth and sophistication has also been part of the West's view of Byzantium.

When the Eastern Empire was in decline and the West began emerging from the Middle Ages, intellectual ties between Italy and Constantinople again became important. Some of the Greek-speaking scholars who served as experts for the Byzantine delegation to the Council of Florence in the late 1440s stayed on to help found the Platonic Academy. The Italian Renaissance and its modern heirs are thus in debt to Byzantine intellectual achievements.

As for the Turks, they have been understood no better than the Byzantines—and admired considerably less. When the Turks became the dominant foreign military threat to Christian Europe, the stereotype in the West was quickly established: cruel and disciplined soldiers with wickedly curved swords; sumptuous seraglios with beautiful harems; a people who lived by treachery, mystery, and sudden violence. When the Turks besieged Vienna in 1529, nearly all of Europe closed ranks to defend Christendom. After the Turkish naval defeat at Lepanto forty-two years later, however, the Turkish Empire seemed less of a menace to the West, and the failure of another siege of Vienna in 1683 confirmed that Turkish civilization and Turkish arms had greatly declined from the glory days of the sixteenth century. In succeeding centuries, the Turkish Empire was fated to become the "Sick Man of Europe," a force manipulated by the great European powers to achieve their own opportunistic ends.

As Turkish fortunes ebbed, exoticism replaced cruelty as the main feature in the West's portrait of Turkey. Things Turkish soon became fashionable in Europe. Even in the twentieth century, the exotic note persists: It was in Moslem Constantinople, that place of opulence and bizarre sexuality, that Virginia Woolf's title character of *Orlando: A Biography* underwent a change from male to female.

All those who would hope to arrive at a more balanced understanding of the Turks and Byzantines must first disabuse themselves of a long succession of such colorful stereotypes. The task is not easy—distortions centuries in the making are not readily abandoned—but the effort is surely worthwhile. For it is only after taking a conscientious look at the histories and cultural achievements of these two peoples that we can gain a legitimate sympathy for two empires which may justifiably be called "monuments of unaging intellect."

RON WILLIAM WALDEN
Department of Religious Studies
Bethany College

Byzantium

Byzantium, the world's first Christian empire, was born out of a miracle. In the year A.D. 312, the future Constantine the Great, approaching Rome and a battle with his rival Maxentius, saw emblazoned in the sky a luminous cross bearing the motto "In this Sign thou shalt conquer."

This vision did not immediately lead to Constantine's conversion to Christianity, but it did inaugu-

rate a new relationship between Roman power and Christian faith. As emperor of Rome, Constantine retained a personal attachment to the sun cult of Mithraism and did not accept baptism until shortly before his death. Yet he did far more than extend passive toleration to the Christians. He gave privileges to the clergy, founded churches, and, above all, called together the church's First Ecumenical Coun-

cil, held at Nicaea in 325. By this last act, Constantine set a precedent, transferring the tradition by which the Roman emperor served as *pontifex maximus,* or chief priest of paganism, to the context of Christianity. From this time on, the supreme secular power of the throne and the spiritual authority of Christendom were to be united in one man.

The veracity of Constantine's miracle has long been questioned by skeptical historians, and indeed there is good reason to suppose that the incident was invented by one of the emperor's biographers. Nevertheless, the tale survives because Constantine's reign was surely, in one sense or another, an inspired one. Under his guidance, Rome turned its face to the East and joined its fate to that of a rising young world religion.

Eighteen years later, in A.D. 330, having defeated his coemperor Licinius, Constantine gave the reconstituted empire a new capital—a "New Rome." The old Rome, with its traditions of senatorial government, had long been thought uncongenial by Constantine's predecessors. Diocletian, for example, had spent only a few weeks of his reign there, preferring to live at Nicomedia in Asia Minor. The selection of a new official capital was still a weighty decision, however. Constantine was thought for a time to have considered Troy, the home of the Romans' legendary ancestor Aeneas. In the end, practicality won out over symbolism. The chosen site was the city of Byzantium, long valued for its strategic location on the Bosporus.

Byzantium, then actually little more than a town, sat on a promontory, which the Turks were later to call "the nose." On the south side of the nose lay the Sea of Marmara, which was connected by the Dardanelles with the Aegean; on the north side lay a long, navigable finger of water known as the Golden Horn; and finally the tip of the nose pointed toward the Bosporus, the straits that led to the Black Sea. In addition to commanding the sea route from the Aegean to the Black Sea, Byzantium was located on the European side of the natural land bridge that, interrupted only by the narrow Bosporus, reached out from eastern Thrace toward Asia Minor.

Preceding page, Justinian the Great presenting a model of the cathedral of Hagia Sophia to the Virgin. Erected in only five years, between A.D. 532 and 537, Hagia Sophia was the grandest of Justinian's many building projects. When the emperor entered the basilica for the consecration ceremonies, he is said to have exclaimed, "Solomon, I have outdone thee!" Above right, a fresco from the church of the Quattro Santi Coronati in Rome, depicting Constantine I granting Pope Sylvester I supreme power over Rome and the West.

Above, Constantine I and his mother, Saint Helena. Of humble origins, Helena made a pilgrimage to Jerusalem in search of holy relics. Below left, Constantinople's aqueduct, built under Valentinian in A.D. 368. Below, the ruins of the monastery of St. John of Studion. The fifth-century church, one of Constantinople's oldest, was a center of the monastic movement.

Two views of the Council of Nicaea: a ninth-century manuscript (left) and a fresco from the church of St. Martin in the Mountains, Rome (above). The choice of Nicaea for this important convocation in A.D. 325 reflected the shift of the balance of power toward the East in the reorganized Christian empire.

Right, the basilica of Hagia Sophia, the site of the Second Council of Nicaea in the eighth century.

Until the coming of Constantine, Byzantium's prominent location had been a mixed blessing at best. Settled about 658 B.C. by Greek colonists from Megara who were led by a commander named Byzas, the city had been conquered by Sparta, besieged unsuccessfully by Philip of Macedon, battered by the local Thracians, and in A.D. 196 razed by the Roman emperor Septimius Severus. In 324, the year Constantine personally paced off the boundaries for his new walled capital, Byzantium's despoiled condition presented him with the opportunity to build almost from scratch.

The new city that he dedicated on May 11, 330, was Roman by design, Greek by tradition, and Christian by destiny. Among its freshly constructed landmarks were a forum; an imperial palace; Roman-style baths; the Hippodrome, where horse races and games took place; and a senate house, though the senate that was to meet there would be strictly an advisory body. Even the homes of the wealthy were often close copies of homes in the old capital, for the upper class was composed almost entirely of families who had followed the emperor from Italy. But New Rome was not exclusively Latin in spirit. To make the city more magnificent, Constantine and his successors filled it with treasures looted

Constantius II (right), the last survivor of the three sons among whom Constantine the Great divided his empire, ruled alone from 350 to 361. Although dedicated to rooting out paganism, Constantius was himself a supporter of the Arian heresy, which denied the full divinity of Christ.

from much of the Greek-speaking East. Like any major Hellenistic city, New Rome had its statue of Tyche and a monument to the Greek god Apollo—though in this case, Apollo's head was replaced by a flattering likeness of Constantine.

In the midst of this Greco-Roman city, there was also evidence of the new state religion. After 330, the building of pagan temples ceased, and Christianity gradually made its presence felt. Among the first Christian treasures of the new capital was a collection of relics assembled by Constantine's mother, Saint Helena, who had made a pilgrimage to the Holy Land. These objects, supposedly dug up by Saint He-

lena on the site of Calvary, included splinters from the True Cross, the Crown of Thorns, and the Lance and Sponge said to have been used by the centurion during the Crucifixion.

Constantine's New Rome soon came to be called Constantinople, while the old Greek name for the city, Byzantium, is today commonly applied to what might more accurately be called the Eastern Roman Empire. This double usage tends to obscure the fact that the people of that time, whom we now refer to as Byzantines, never thought of themselves as such. Although they were a mixed lot ethnically and although they came from a variety of cultural backgrounds, the

Above, the marble base of the Egyptian obelisk that Theodosius I erected on the racecourse of the Hippodrome. A detail of the carved reliefs (right) shows the emperor, his family, and his court receiving tribute from conquered barbarians.

Below, a coin bearing the portrait of Theodosius I. From the time of Constantine, the gold solidus, weighing 4.54 grams, was the mainstay of Byzantine coinage. Left, a view of the walls of Constantinople.

citizens of Byzantium considered themselves Romans. After about the sixth century, when Greek replaced Latin as the chief language of the empire, their name was simply translated into the Greek *Romaioi*.

The precise moment at which the old Roman Empire ceased and Byzantium began is more a historical convenience than an accurate reflection of the period of change and transition that marked the first two centuries after the death of Constantine. Constantine's immediate successors did not even live in his new capital, and the last of his family, the scholarly Julian the Apostate, devoted his brief rule to a futile campaign to restore paganism.

The major threat to the empire by this time, however, was not paganism but the attacks of the barbarians, especially the Goths, who were being pushed southward from Germany by waves of advancing

The walls of Constantinople, expanded under the emperor Theodosius II in the fifth century, protected the "God-guarded City" of Constantinople for a thousand years. Portions of the walls (left and on facing page) are still standing today. Above, the Golden Door, which was the assembly point for triumphal processions.

Huns. In 378, the troops of the emperor Gratian suffered a serious defeat at Adrianople, and it looked for a time as if Constantinople itself might fall. Eventually, though, the Eastern commanders successfully assimilated the Goths by turning them into mercenaries. By the mid-fifth century, the Gothic general Aspar was briefly the power behind the imperial throne, and it seemed possible that the Goths would come to dominate the empire by peaceful means.

The western half of the empire, meanwhile, had been ruled separately since 395, when the will of the emperor Theodosius I had confirmed the division of Rome between his two sons. By far weaker than the East, the West eventually bore the brunt of the barbarian incursions. When the last Western emperor was deposed in 476 by the Ostrogoth king Odoacer, the event was regarded in Constantinople as tragic though hardly surprising in view of the East's failure

to send aid. It was by no means considered the fall of the Roman Empire.

The idea that Rome "fell" in A.D. 476 is one of a number of parochial notions that make it difficult for persons educated in the Western European tradition to see Byzantium for what it was. Prejudices centuries in the making are not easily eradicated, and no doubt there are still some who would secretly sympathize with the nineteenth-century historian W. H. Leckie, who complained, in his *History of European Morals,* that Byzantine history was one long chronicle of decadence and debauchery. Of the Byzantine Empire, Leckie wrote:

The universal verdict of history is that it constitutes with scarcely an exception, the most thoroughly base and despicable form that civilization has yet assumed. . . . The history of the Empire is a monot-

Above, an ivory diptych of the Vandal general Stilicho. On his deathbed, Theodosius I had divided his empire between his two sons, Arcadius and Honorius, but Stilicho soon became the de facto ruler of Honorius' Western domains. He was called from Italy to lead the defense of the Eastern Empire against the Visigoth king Alaric and later fought Alaric in Italy as well. Two years after Stilicho's death in 408, Rome was looted and burned.

onous story of the intrigues of priests, eunuchs and women, of poisoning and conspiracies, of uniform ingratitude and perpetual fratricides.

Leckie's view of Byzantine history is only partially accurate: Byzantium was essentially a fortress empire, fated to be ever on the defensive against successive waves of invaders—Germans, Persians, Arabs, Slavs, Turks, and so on. But the rest is far from the truth. During most of the Middle Ages, the Byzantines were richer, better educated, and more civilized than their counterparts in the West, but there is no reason to believe that they were any more immoral. Their seemingly endless religious disputes were no more senseless than, say, the Inquisition. And their bureaucracy, far from being the ineffective and cumbersome caste system that some believe it to have been, was actually strikingly effective.

The basic features of Byzantine society, both admirable and not so admirable, were well established during the reign of Justinian I, also known as Justinian the Great because of his many accomplishments. Inheriting the throne from his uncle Justin I in 527, Justinian was only two generations removed from his peasant origins. His empress, Theodora, was also of humble birth. The daughter of a Hippodrome bear trainer, she was rumored to have begun her career as an actress and courtesan. She especially has been much maligned by a scandalous secret history attributed to the scholar Procopius. But rather than providing evidence of decadence, the ability of these two parvenus to ascend the throne may be taken as proof of the vitality of a society in which birth often counted for less than ambition and talent. Once in power, both Justinian and Theodora proved to be remarkably competent.

A curious aspect of political life in Constantinople was the connection between civic politics and the circus. The source of attraction was the Hippodrome chariot races, so avidly followed by the people of the city that rival racing factions, the Blues and the Greens, eventually grew into armed militias and, in a crude sense, political parties. Young blades dressed for the games in flamboyant costumes and adopted a characteristic hair style, shaving their heads in front while allowing their locks to grow out long in the back. When the factions tired of cheering on their favorites and making wagers, they roamed the streets, sometimes attacking unwary pedestrians.

The Blues had for some time been the imperial party, but by 532 both factions were dissatisfied with Justinian's imposition of high taxes and his autocratic

Below, two coins, the upper one from the reign of Arcadius' son Theodosius II, and the lower one, a coin with a portrait of the emperor Zeno, whose reign was marred by revolt and saw the overthrow of the last Western emperor, Romulus Augustulus. Zeno's successor, Anastasius I, represented by one of his edicts (left) was forced to negotiate with the barbarians. An able administrator, Anastasius perfected the empire's monetary system and proved confident in dealing with both domestic and foreign issues. His beliefs in Monophysitism, however, caused periodic unrest and uprisings among his subjects.

Arcadius (left) was an ineffective ruler whose quarrels with Stilicho only hastened the decline of the West.

MAXIMIANVS

disregard of their opinions. In January of that year, the emperor's rather clumsy attempt to put down a demonstration in the Hippodrome led to an outburst of rioting and arson known as the Nika rebellion— "Nika," or "Victory!" being the rallying cry raised by the factions as they ran through the streets murdering and looting. Even when Justinian offered to dismiss several of his most unpopular officials, the factions refused to disperse, and the emperor became panicky. With as much as a quarter of the city in flames, Justinian and his loyal advisers prepared to flee, but at the last minute, Theodora changed their minds by declaring her own conviction that she would rather die an empress than live as an exile. "The purple," she concluded resolutely, "makes an excellent shroud." With this example before them, Justinian and his supporters took heart, and the general Beli-

sarius led a detachment of troops to the Hippodrome, where they caught the rioters in the midst of their drunken victory celebration. Blocking the exits, they massacred thousands.

The suppression of the Nika rebellion left Justinian in a stronger position than ever. Theodora's courage was the perfect foil for Justinian's industry, and his greatest accomplishments were launched after the threat of rebellion subsided. An enthusiastic builder, Justinian began immediately to reconstruct his capital. The most ambitious project was his commissioning of Anthemius of Tralles and Isidorus of Miletus to create a new church, Hagia Sophia, which was finished in only five years. The church's great dome was celebrated as the most daring structure of its kind in Christendom—so daring that it collapsed some twenty years later and had to be reconstructed along

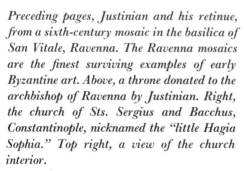

Preceding pages, Justinian and his retinue, from a sixth-century mosaic in the basilica of San Vitale, Ravenna. The Ravenna mosaics are the finest surviving examples of early Byzantine art. Above, a throne donated to the archbishop of Ravenna by Justinian. Right, the church of Sts. Sergius and Bacchus, Constantinople, nicknamed the "little Hagia Sophia." Top right, a view of the church interior.

less ambitious lines. Despite this accident, Hagia Sophia, the Church of the Holy Wisdom, was built to last: It is still standing some fourteen hundred and fifty years later.

Justinian's other lasting accomplishment was the *Corpus juris civilis,* a codification and revision of the body of Roman law. Justinian's code did not abolish slavery, a move that had been suggested more than a century earlier by the radical churchman Saint John Chrysostom, the "Golden-mouthed." But it did strengthen the family, forbidding parents to sell their children into bondage and guaranteeing a widow's right to become the guardian of her children. Later emperors revised Justinian's laws to align them further with Christian principles.

Justinian's achievements extended into the military realm as well. In the reconquest of Italy from the

Two portraits from the age of Justinian: above, a philosopher portrayed in a mosaic from the imperial palace; right, a statue of an officer or magistrate.

Byzantine Empire at the beginning of Justinian's reign

Justinian's conquests

The fortunes of Byzantium

Because of its central geographical location, the Byzantine Empire developed into a major cultural and historical crossroads. Culturally, Byzantium acted as a bridge between Europe and Asia and between the classical world and the world of the Renaissance. Historically, the fortunes of the empire are inseparably bound up with the achievements and failures of numerous peoples in both Europe and Asia.

The empire was at war during much of the reign of Justinian the Great (527–565). After North Africa fell to Justinian's army in 533 and 534, the emperor turned his attention to the Italian peninsula. Italy's defeat culminated in the capture of Ravenna (540), the last stronghold in the north. Although Justinian's forces subsequently lost part of Italy, including Rome, to the Goth general Totila, by 554 all of Italy was once again under total Byzantine control.

The period known as the Macedonian era (867–1025) began when Basil I murdered Michael III and assumed the throne. During this time, Byzantium enjoyed a golden age. The military reasserted its power over the Arabs in the East, various Slavic tribes were brought into the Byzantine sphere through conversion to Christianity, and interest in scholarship was revived. This period also witnessed a rise in monasticism and a growing concern with the ownership of land, which was concentrated in the hands of a few powerful families. Basil II, the last emperor of this era, attempted to deal with the land situation by ordering harsh sanctions against the landed aristocracy and demanding restitution to the peasants, but after his death in 1025 the wealthy landowners struck back successfully.

Byzantium in the eleventh century was racked by internal strife. Tensions arose between military leaders in the provinces and civil leaders in Constantinople, each

Latin Empire of Constantinople
Byzantine Empire of Nicaea
Byzantine Empire of Trebizond
Despotate of Epirus

group putting forth its own candidate for emperor. Trouble appeared on the frontiers of Byzantium as well. The Pechenegs, a Turkic tribe, crossed the Danube into Byzantium and proved to be a menace to peace for some time to come. The Seljuk Turks entered the empire from the east in 1065 and reached as far as Nicaea by 1081. The Normans pounded Byzantium from the west, and in 1071 the last Byzantine stronghold in Italy came under Norman rule. A decisive blow was dealt to Byzantium during the Fourth Crusade. In retaliation for an anti-Western uprising in Constantinople some twenty years before, the Crusaders sacked the city on April 13, 1204. The event marked the end of a glorious era.

From the sack of Constantinople by the Crusaders until the Turkish siege of 1453, the Byzantine Empire was ruled by a succession of emperors who desperately attempted to manage its affairs. Michael VIII, who was crowned emperor in August 1261, took steps to insure that his reign would be successful. He tried to revive the empire's sluggish trade and began to refortify Constantinople. He met with resistance, however, when he attempted to reunite the Church of Constantinople with the Holy See in Rome. Branded a heretic and a traitor, he died in 1282. Michael's son Andronicus II ruled from 1282 to 1328. During his reign the empire, although plagued by financial difficulties, experienced a cultural and spiritual renaissance. Andronicus' grandson Andronicus III assumed the throne in 1328, but it was John Cantacuzene, a young aristocrat, who actually guided the empire's policies. When Andronicus III died in 1341, civil war broke out; five years later, John Cantacuzene was crowned Emperor John VI.

The era following John VI's reign was marked by Turkish expansion. Byzantium became a vassal state of the Turks and was forced to pay tribute to the Ottoman sultan. During the reign of Manuel II, who assumed the throne in 1391, Byzantium enjoyed a respite from the Turks. This period was short-lived, however, for at this point the empire had neither external support nor its own means for long-term survival. The final blow occurred on May 29, 1453, when soldiers of Mohammed II stormed their way through the walls of Constantinople.

The Hippodrome

Like the Romans of classical times, the people of Constantinople were avid devotees of circuses and chariot races. Organized factions of racing fans, known collectively as the *demes,* eventually became the basis of the civil militia and the voice of the people in political matters. Reigning emperors presided over the Hippodrome games, and spokesmen for the factions sometimes used such occasions to present popular grievances. Although the factions had no power to elect officials, they served as rallying points for popular opinion, and the emperor ignored them at his peril.

The Hippodrome itself was modeled after the Circus Maximus in Rome and was one of Constantinople's oldest structures. Seating sixty thousand spectators, it contained a race course decorated with ancient statuary, including an obelisk brought by Theodosius I from Egypt and a bronze column of intertwined serpents transported from Delphi.

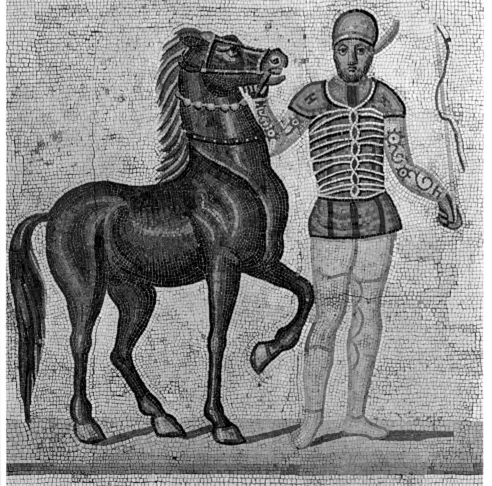

Racing at the Hippodrome was originally organized around four competing teams: Greens, Whites, Reds, and Blues (left, below, and on facing page—left to right). By the time of Justinian the Great, the Whites and Reds had died out, leading to a two-way rivalry between the Blues, whose supporters were identified with the aristocracy and the Orthodox religion, and the Greens, who favored the Monophysites and, to some extent, spoke for the lower classes. Sports and politics proved to be a volatile combination. Justinian the Great's attempt to control factional violence led both sides to unite against him in the Nika rebellion of A.D. 532.

Above, another view of the chariot races, from an ivory diptych of the fifth century.

Above, a fresco showing a race of four-horse chariots. This was the predominant form of racing. However, two-horse chariots, bareback riding, and so-called Roman-style riding, in which the jockey stood astride a pair of horses, were also popular.

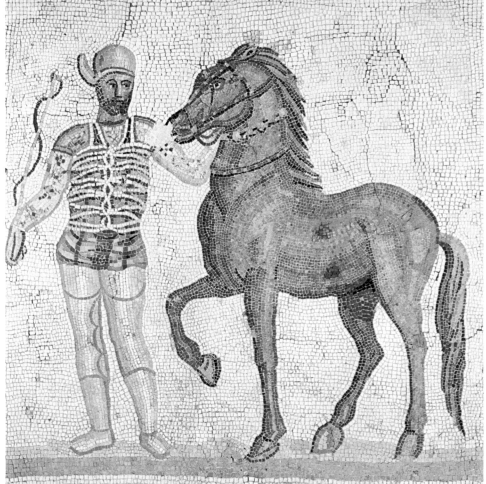

Justinian: Byzantium's lawgiver

Justinian (left) is shown surrounded by soldiers and jurists in this illustration from an edition of his Institutions, *a handbook for law students and teachers.*

Byzantium was an absolute autocracy. Under the doctrine of caesaropapism, supreme power over both church and state was vested in the person of the *basileus autocrator,* or emperor. The emperor promulgated the laws; he in turn was guided by the spirit of the law.

Justinian I, in attempting to reorganize obsolete and confusing Roman statutes, declared himself to be guided by the principles of "humanity, common sense, and public utility." The improved position of women under Justinian's new code is usually attributed to the influence of his wife Theodora. Certain practices were outlawed by the code on the grounds that the "just opinion of modern society" condemned their harshness. Above all, crimes were clearly defined and procedures established to protect the rights of the accused. The civil courts were held in high respect. Because of them the conflicts between canon and civil law that so frequently figured in western European history seldom arose in Byzantium.

Left, a spearhead used by Justinian for ceremonial purposes.

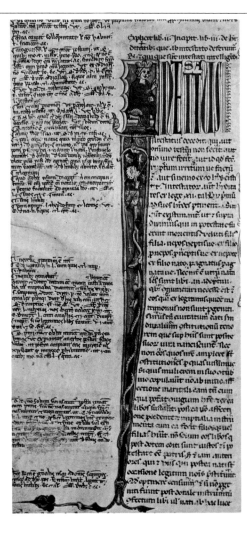

Immediately above and left, two illuminated pages from various editions of the Corpus juris civilis. *Fortunately, this work has been preserved almost in its entirety.*

Above, Justinian dictating his laws, in a miniature from a tenth-century codex. In the immense labor of reorganizing the old Roman laws, Justinian was aided by a commission of scholars organized under the quaestor Tribonian. Left, Justinian's monogram on the Bucholeon gate in Constantinople.

Goths, Justinian made use of the services of two brilliant generals, both of whom fought bitter and extended campaigns with inadequate support of men and supplies. The first of these generals was Belisarius, who had quelled the Nika rebellion and had retaken Carthage from the barbarians in a surprise attack. He was sent to Italy in 535, where it was rumored that the Ostrogoths had offered to surrender Ravenna to him only if he would become their king. Belisarius remained loyal to his emperor, but his popularity aroused jealousy in Constantinople. Called home and stripped of his command, Belisarius nevertheless returned to defend the empire against the Bulgars in 559. His place in Italy was taken by his rival, the eunuch Narses, who oversaw the return to Byzantine rule in 554; he commanded well, though many were shocked by the appointment of a eunuch to a military post.

Justinian was such an industrious ruler that he became known to his subjects as "he who never sleeps." In fact, hard-working emperors were the rule rather than the exception in Byzantium. The notion that the emperor could have too much authority or that the state could be overregulated would never have occurred to a Byzantine. Taxes, wages, customs duties, prices, profits, and land transfers all came under the close scrutiny of the imperial administration, and the emperor, as supreme head of state, was ultimately responsible for signing all documents in purple ink. Partly owing to such responsibilities, the emperor rarely had occasion to leave Constantinople unless he was leading a military campaign; until the twelfth century, emperors spent most of their time within the walls of the palace.

Members of the imperial family were generally granted high-sounding titles. It had become the custom to elevate recognized heirs to the status of co-emperor, with the ruling sovereign arrogating to himself the supreme title of *basileus autocrator*. If an emperor was incompetent or uninterested in his official duties, the coemperor might exercise effective power. Usually, though, the palace affairs were seen to by the emperor himself, aided by officials who were likely to be eunuchs. The fashion for eunuchs at court had begun before Constantine, and was perpetuated in the belief that such men, having no heirs, would be loyal to the interests of the imperial family. So important did eunuchs become that some ambitious families actually had one or more sons castrated in the hope that the boys would reach a high rank at court and be in a favored position to advance their interests.

Ceremony, the visible expression of the Byzantine faith in regulation, took up a considerable portion of

Byzantine mosaics, manuscripts, and paintings provide us with a record of many long-vanished monuments. This twelfth-century miniature depicting the church of the Holy Apostles in Constantinople (far left) is the only surviving picture of this sixth-century basilica. Two mosaics from Sant'Apollinare Nuovo in Ravenna show the town of Ravenna and the port of Classe (above) and the palace of Theodoric (left). Below, a vision of Heavenly Jerusalem from San Vitale, Ravenna.

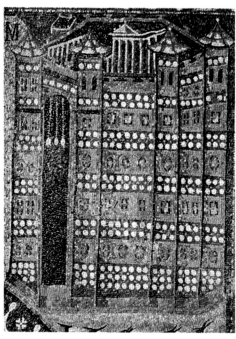

the emperor's time. His people loved a good show, and the activities of the court appear to have been savored for their pomp and pageantry. Elaborately dressed, his facial expressions hidden behind a mask of make-up, the emperor was the central figure in the carefully staged diplomatic audiences. Emissaries from less civilized countries were sometimes awed by displays of mechanical toys, while the more sophisticated would be shown gold and jeweled icons. Yet, such audiences did not exhaust the emperor's ceremonial duties. He was also expected to preside over the games at the Hippodrome and to participate in any number of church rites. On Easter, for example, the emperor would appear at mass wrapped in white bandages and escorted by twelve men representing the disciples of Christ.

Because the Eastern Church was essentially an arm of the state, the emperor also had a stake in making sure that his subjects remained within the Orthodox fold. As a result, heresy was a political crime. But interest in theological questions was never something that had to be imposed from above. Ordinary men and women lived in the hope of one day reaching heaven, and, especially in Constantinople, doctrinal disputes were avidly followed by the man in the street. This phenomenon was as startling to travelers of that time as it is today, and Gregory of Nyssa, writing in the late fourth century of a visit to the capital, noted with some pique that

> if you ask someone how many obols a thing costs, he replies by dogmatizing on the born and the unborn. If you ask the price of bread, they answer you, the Father is greater than the Son, and the Son is subordinate to Him. If you ask, Is my bath ready, they answer you, the Son has been made out of nothing.

During the early centuries of the empire, theological arguments centered around one especially knotty question: How could it be said that Christ was both human and divine? The principals in the quarrel were often the rival theologians of Antioch and Alexandria—then the two most powerful cities of eastern Byzantium. The Alexandrines favored theories that

Mosaics from Justinian I's Great Palace reflect the Hellenistic tradition of using such works to decorate the walls and floors of secular buildings. Left, from top to bottom: children riding on camels, two hunters armed with spears, and the head of a soldier. Facing page, top left and right, two views of the monastery church of Alahan in Cilicia, a well-preserved example of mid-fifth-century architecture. Right, the walls of Gerapolis in Asia Minor.

Saint John Chrysostom (above far right) was an eloquent preacher and champion of the poor. The church of St. John, Ephesus (right), is a twentieth-century reconstruction of the original, built by Justinian and Theodora over the tomb of Saint John the Evangelist. The crypt of the church of the Seven Sleepers (below far right) was a popular burial place; seven martyrs of Ephesus were said to have awakened there after two hundred years of repose.

Above, a page from an illustrated book of the Gospels produced in the monastery of Zagba, Mesopotamia, showing two monks in a typically oriental temple. Right, Saint Gregory of Nyssa, one of the four principal church fathers of Orthodox Christianity.

emphasized the unity between the divine and the human in Christ, while the Antiochenes wanted to protect the distinction between the two. The view that finally prevailed, the one we now call Orthodox, combined features of both schools. In a succession of ecumenical councils, the Orthodox party, usually under the emperor's patronage, settled on a delicate and subtle compromise: Christ had two separate "natures," human and divine, but was only one "person." Along the way, the councils condemned extreme positions, both Antiochene and Alexandrine, as heresies.

Of course, many nontheological passions were caught up in the religious battles. The entire empire was convulsed when Nestorius, a fifth-century abbot of Antioch who had become patriarch of Constantinople, was condemned for heresy, deposed, and exiled—all for believing that Christ not only had two natures but was two persons. The Alexandrine reaction was almost predictable: Christ not only was just one person, but he had only one nature. This view, called Monophysitism, was condemned as heretical in its turn.

The main lines of the Orthodox doctrine of Christ were established by the end of the Fourth Ecumenical Council, held at Chalcedon in 451, but Monophysi-

tism refused to die. The view prevailed, especially in the eastern territories of the empire, where it became a rallying point for the grievances of the empire's Syrian and Egyptian subjects. By Justinian's time, the quarrel had reached the royal household itself. The emperor, who fancied himself a theologian in his own right, was unconvinced by the Monophysite position; also, he was aware that its spread could undermine his campaign to maintain his authority over the patriarch (or pope) of Rome. On the other hand, Theodora, having already traveled in the East before she became empress, managed to persuade Justinian to appoint as patriarch of Constantinople a holy man,

Anthimius, who was sympathetic to the Monophysite cause. This ploy failed, and Anthimius was soon replaced, but the empress managed to hide him away in the women's quarters of the palace, where he remained until he was discovered after Theodora's death.

Justinian never recovered from Theodora's passing. He devoted more and more of his time to trying to find a theological solution to the Monophysite question and ended by slipping into a complicated heresy himself. Upon his death in A.D. 565, his successors adopted what seemed to be a sensible policy of retrenchment, attempting to solidify his accomplish-

Women in Byzantium

After the coming of Christianity, the rights that Byzantine women enjoyed were strengthened. Divorce was possible though discouraged, and a widow was assured of her right to act as head of the household.

In general, the roles of men and women were sharply differentiated in Byzantium. Wealthier women spent much of their time in the *gynacaeum*, or women's quarters of the house—though they were by no means confined there. Byzantium's tradition of social mobility gave women considerable leeway. Sex, like class, was a barrier that could sometimes be transcended.

Learned women appear frequently in the annals of Byzantine history. Anna Comnena's chronicle of her father's reign is among the landmarks of Byzantine scholarship. A woman doctor is listed as a staff member of a twelfth-century hospital in Constantinople. And the ninth-century poet Casia was known as one of the wittiest writers of her age.

Below, a fourth-century mosaic, now displayed in the Archaeological Museum of Antioch. Below right, a woman's face depicted in enamel on a gold earring.

Left, virgins of the tribe of David. This scene is from a mosaic in the Kariye Camii of Constantinople, formerly the church of the Savior in Chora. The women's long tunics and shawls are typical of ceremonial dress in late Byzantine times; in contrast to the rough linen and wool of classical attire, Byzantine costumes were made of silks and other rich fabrics. Above, the head of Soteria, the symbol of salvation.

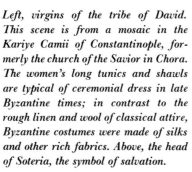

A servant woman carrying an amphora (above) appears in the genre mosaics of the imperial palace in Constantinople. Left, a woman preparing a cradle in anticipation of the birth of the Virgin Mary. This detail from the Kariye Camii is part of a series depicting the life of the Virgin.

The rise of Islam

A.D. 622, the year the emperor Heraclius set out to crush the might of the Sassanid Persians once and for all, was coincidentally the same year that the prophet Mohammed fled from Mecca to Medina. This event in remote Arabia, which marked the beginning of the Moslem era, would seem to have been of little import to Byzantium.

Within Heraclius' own lifetime, however, a Moslem army led by Khalid, the "Sword of Allah," swept into Byzantine-ruled Jordan, Syria, Palestine, and Egypt.

The sudden rise of a Moslem empire in the very homeland of Christianity stunned the Byzantine Empire, but religious quarrels among Christians had in fact already laid the groundwork for the Moslem conquest. Many Christians who had been made to endure the persecutions of the Orthodox clergy of Constantinople saw Islam as a lesser evil. A Christian community nonetheless survived within the Islamic

Empire for centuries, despite periodic attempts at suppression.

Although Byzantium and the Arab caliphates were bitter enemies in war, there was a more peaceful side to contacts between the two. For example, Greek architects and masons played a significant role in the construction of the Omayyad caliphs' capital at Damascus, and Egyptian and Syrian Christians served the Moslems as artists, educators, and administrators. Arab learning, which later stimulated the European Renaissance, thus owed an early debt to the Byzantines.

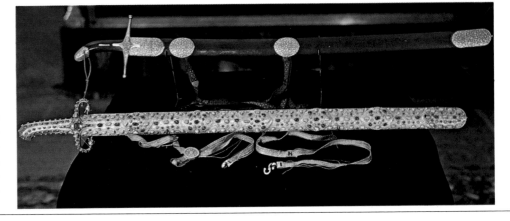

Relics of Mohammed preserved today in the Topkapi Museum, Istanbul, include an ark containing the Prophet's cloak (above), his sword (right), and a tooth encased in a reliquary (facing page, below left). A miniature (above right) shows Mohammed leading his faithful followers to the conquest of Mecca in 630.

Above, the prophet Mohammed ascending to heaven after his death in 632, in a detail from a miniature by Ahmed Musa. Within a year, Moslem armies had begun their holy war against the infidels. Right, Moslem general Khalid among a group of pilgrims visiting the shrine of the sacred black stone, the Kaaba, in Mecca.

During the early centuries of the Byzantine Empire, fine textiles often featured scenes of hunting, portraits of the emperors, or episodes and personages from sacred history, such as the Apostles (above). After Justinian's time, when the secrets of silk cultivation had been stolen from the East, oriental motifs and stylized figures (below) became popular.

ments and, above all, to ease the financial strain Justinian's policies had placed on the administration and its subjects. Despite their praiseworthy goals, they accomplished little. Justin II, Justinian's nephew, soon went mad under the strain of office and spent his days being pulled about the palace in a wheeled cart. Even Maurice, the most competent ruler of the period, was eventually dethroned and killed by his troops, the result of their dissatisfaction with his demands and his isolationist policy. Rather than accompanying them into battle, Maurice chose to remain in Constantinople. Consequently, he enjoys the distinction of being the first Byzantine emperor to be murdered by a usurper—a junior officer who became Phocas I. Under this traitor, the state teetered on the brink of anarchy.

Just when the situation seemed darkest, Byzantium found its savior. In A.D. 610, the popular general Heraclius, son of the governor of Carthage, sailed into the Golden Horn and took over the reins of the demoralized government. Although a formidable leader, Heraclius was no superman, and he struggled to avert total collapse. In 614, the Sassanid Persians sacked Jerusalem, an event that sent shock waves through the Christian world. By 616, the Persians were in Egypt, and the barbarian Avars were overrunning the Balkans and threatening to attack Constantinople. At one point, Heraclius decided to abandon the capital for Carthage. His ships were already loaded for the voyage when a public outcry, led by the outraged patriarch Sergius, caused him to relent. Taking advantage of a promise of financial support from the Church, Heraclius built up the imperial army and in 622 marched against the Persians. Five years later, he won a decisive victory over the Sassanid emperor Chosroes II in a battle fought near the plain of Gaugamela—the site of Alexander the Great's triumph over Darius III.

Heraclius is traditionally credited with the development of the so-called *theme* system, an arrangement by which the military and civil administration of a region was combined and soldiers living in specified districts received small grants of land in exchange for their service under arms. This land could be passed on to an heir, provided he too served in the imperial army. The theme system encouraged the army to meddle in politics, but it created, especially in Asia Minor and Armenia, a dependable source of loyal troops who were to serve the empire well throughout troubled centuries to come.

In spite of his many triumphs, Heraclius died in 641, a broken and dispirited man. He had conquered the Persians and in 629 personally led the solemn

Above, an Arabic painting on glass depicting a scene from the Romance of Antar, a historical work that weaves together a series of legendary or traditional episodes. Below, a coin, and right, a jeweled cross—both dating from the reign of Justinian's nephew Justin II. The cross, a reliquary supposedly containing a splinter of the True Cross, was presented by Justin to the Vatican.

procession restoring the True Cross to the city of Jerusalem. Yet shortly thereafter the Holy Land was threatened by even more formidable invaders—the Arabs. Before his death in 632, the prophet Mohammed is said to have sent a message to Heraclius, inviting him to convert to Islam or face the consequences. The suggestion must have seemed pure presumption at the time but proved to be a prophetic warning: Arab armies soon swept into Syria, took Damascus, and in 637 established themselves in Jerusalem. This time, the True Cross vanished forever.

Ironically, considering the Arabs' reputation in the West for proselytizing by the sword, their advance through Syria and into Egypt was often welcomed by the Monophysite populations, who found the Islamic conquerors more tolerant than their own Orthodox brothers in Constantinople. The pro-Western policies of the imperial administration had left deep scars,

Above, a solidus showing the emperor Heraclius with his son, later Constantine III, in the background. Below left, Heraclius in a triumphant warrior pose. This linen-wool fabric probably comes from an Egyptian tunic of the seventh or eighth century.

Left, Constantinople during the Avar siege of 626, shown in a detail from a sixteenth-century fresco in the Church of the Moldavita monastery, Bucovina, Romania. Below right, Avar arrowheads and spearheads.

preoccupied with the old problem of the barbarians, who by now included the Slavs, the Khazars, and the Bulgars. Justinian II followed the established Byzantine policy of pacifying those barbarians who could not be exterminated. He himself was married to a Khazar princess, and he defused the Slavic threat by resettling thousands of Slavic families in Asia Minor, where they settled down to become model farmers.

In Constantinople, Justinian II's exorbitant taxation, combined with his personal sadism, made him highly unpopular. In 695, the general Leontius staged a successful revolt, and Justinian was driven into exile—after first having his nose cut off and his tongue split, disfigurements that won him the name "Rhinotmetus" ("Cut-off Nose") and were meant to insure that he would henceforth stay out of the public eye. But Leontius was also in an unfortunate position, being in power at the time of the fall of Carthage, an event that sparked a mutiny within the Byzantine armed forces. As a result, he met with a fate similar to Justinian's, and was replaced by the general Tiberius Apsimar, who took the throne as Tiberius III in 698.

Constantinople had not seen the last of Justinian. After a decade in exile, he returned home at the head of a Bulgar army and, reassuming the throne, staged a bizarre ceremony in the Hippodrome, during which he sat with one foot upon the neck of each of his two successors while the crowd was urged to chant a verse from the Ninety-first Psalm, "Thou shalt tread upon the lion and the adder." To Justinian's mind, the double pun on the names of his enemies (Leo means lion and Apsimar sounds like asp) must have seemed brilliant. But the slaughter that followed was anything but amusing, and when his opponents managed to stage a second revolt six years later, they did not stop at mutilation. Justinian and his infant son were

and in hindsight it seems that the fall of the eastern provinces was a blessing in disguise, freeing Constantinople from the burden of governing provinces it did not understand and could never properly control. Of course, the Arab advance hardly seemed to have any saving graces at the time. Fired by their success—and by the belief that the fall of Byzantium would set the stage for the end of the world—the Arabs set their sights on the utter destruction of New Rome. Twice in fifty years—in 678 and again during 717 and 718—they besieged Constantinople itself. The Arab advance seemed irresistible, but even these soldiers could not prevail against the impregnable fortress city of Constantinople.

Nonetheless, the Arab threat was by no means ended. Moslem armies moved across North Africa, and Carthage, home city of the Heraclian dynasty, fell in 698. The successors of Heraclius, however, were

slaughtered, and the Heraclian dynasty came to an end.

This sorry episode left Constantinople without effective leadership during the very years when the Arabs were preparing for a second attack on the city. Then, in A.D. 717, another emperor of humble birth, Leo III, the Isaurian, came into power. Leo, who was probably from Syria and not Isauria in Asia Minor, had risen through the ranks of the imperial service. He spoke Arabic as fluently as he spoke Greek, and he may have come to power because he had the secret support of the Arabs, who believed they could make him their puppet. Nothing could have been further from the truth.

The second siege of Constantinople proved to be far more costly for the Arabs than the first. As before, Greek fire—an incendiary mixture used to set enemy

ships ablaze—was a formidable weapon, but this time, the Byzantines were also aided by the weather. The winter of 717–718 was especially severe, and the Arab armies encamped around Constantinople were caught unprepared. As many as 150,000 out of 180,000 died. Western histories typically describe the battle of Tours in 732 as the high point of Arab expansionism, but the year 718 was equally significant. If Constantinople had fallen, there would have been little to prevent enormous Arab armies from pushing into the heart of Europe.

Even more than Heraclius, Leo III deserves to be remembered as the savior of Byzantium. Yet, his name is most often associated with a violent religious dispute that began during his reign and wracked his dynasty—the Iconoclastic controversy. Leo became convinced, perhaps by a volcanic eruption on the island of Santorin in 726, that God was angry with

Byzantium and that the cause of His fury was the veneration of sacred images, or icons. Leo ordered the great mosaic of Christ that stood on the Chalke gate of the imperial palace to be torn down, and four years later he extended his policy to the churches themselves. Mosaics were whitewashed or destroyed, icons were burned, and even coins bearing religious images were melted down. Many pious folk did their best to protect the holy pictures they loved, and the progress of the imperial troops who traveled through the empire smashing icons was attended by widespread civil disturbances.

Numerous theories have been advanced to explain the passionate confrontation between Iconoclasts and Iconodules—"image breakers" and "image venerators." On the most basic level, the controversy was a religious one. The use of representational objects in

The central role of Hagia Sophia in the life of Constantinople is indicated by the prominence of the church in this fifteenth-century Florentine map (facing page, below left). The dome, about ninety-three feet across, is set over a circlet of windows, so that it seems to float above the thick exterior walls (facing page, above left). Facing page, right, a detail of the façade. In the interior (three views on this page), natural light on rich marbles and open arcades creates a mood of mystical calm.

Christian worship was an ancient practice, and the popular mind associated it with the veneration of saints' relics. Nonetheless, icons bred superstition. Many of them were the subject of elaborate legends connecting them to the church fathers, and some, reputedly not made by human hands, were thought to have the power to work miracles. Pious Byzantines were even known to nominate icons as godparents for their children.

On another level, Iconoclasm was a reaction against the monasteries, which were strongholds of icon veneration. Because of their role in spreading literacy and preserving scholarly traditions, the monasteries of Western Europe are remembered today as guardians of culture. In the East, monks served many of the same functions as their Western counterparts. They copied manuscripts, dispensed charity, and fed pilgrims and travelers. Nevertheless, the place of the monasteries in society was somewhat different, and by the eighth century, their growing wealth and influence aroused the envy of the state itself.

Fear that the monasteries would become independent centers of power surfaced as early as 451, when the Council of Chalcedon warned, "There are some . . . who make the monastic life an excuse for causing trouble in the churches and in political affairs." This viewpoint was finally borne out in the seventh century, by which time the wealth and influence of the monks had become impressive. Large land grants, both from the imperial family and from private individuals, made the monasteries rich and removed valuable properties from the tax rolls. As for the numbers of people seeking to enter religious communities, estimates vary, but monks and nuns certainly formed a substantial and growing proportion of the population. The economic impact of the movement, combined with the substantial influence of the monks over the uneducated populace, made monasticism seem threatening indeed.

Leo III's son Constantine V, known to his enemies as Copronymous, or "the Dung-named," was an especially ardent foe of the monks. During his reign (741–775), monks were drafted into the army, forced to marry nuns, and marshaled for humiliating cere-

Above, an illustration from a tenth-century manuscript in which Christ is shown crowning Constantine VI and his wife. Right, a medal showing Leo III, the Isaurian.

monies in which they were made to march through the Hippodrome hand in hand with women. Oddly enough, Constantine married his son and heir to an icon venerator and friend of monasticism, Irene, who came from a noble family in Athens. The marriage appears to have been a happy one, but Irene's husband soon died and she, left to serve as regent for their young son, gave Byzantium its icons once again.

Irene eventually became the first woman to rule the empire in her own right, signing imperial documents with the male title "basileus." The methods by which she came to the throne, culminating in the blinding and murder of her son Constantine VI, were hardly

admirable. But the army, whose soldiers were drawn largely from regions in Asia Minor, was still strongly pro-Iconoclast, and Irene seems to have had reason to believe that her irresolute son was about to deliver the empire back into the hands of a party she considered heretical.

The Iconoclastic reaction had placed a great strain on Byzantium's relationship with Christians in western Europe, which was uniformly Iconodule. The appearance of a woman on the imperial throne, despite the fact that she was not an Iconoclast, now provided an excuse for Pope Leo III to express his estrangement by crowning Charlemagne, king of the Franks, emperor of the Romans on Christmas Day, 800. Charlemagne himself was not really powerful enough to be a significant military threat to Byzantium. In fact, he was eager for a diplomatic alliance and even sought to marry the now aged Irene. The papal attitude was another matter. As early as 756, Pope Stephen's alliance with the Frankish king Pepin had re-

Above left, the Second Council of Nicaea, as depicted in a painting now in the Royal Museum, Copenhagen. The council was called in 787 to consider the Iconoclast question. Above, an ivory diptych of Ariadne, widow of the emperor Zeno and wife of Anastasius. Right, the interior of Hagia Irene, the church of Holy Peace. Built as a companion to Hagia Sophia, the church was extensively remodeled after an earthquake in 740.

sulted in the transfer into the papal domains of the exarchate of Ravenna, which had been Byzantium's last piece of territory in northern Italy until it had fallen to the Lombards in 751. Now the pope was claiming the right to name a Roman emperor. Since, in theory, there could be only one Roman emperor at a time, this claim was viewed unfavorably by the Byzantines.

The papacy's presumption was made even more explicit by the appearance of a document known as the Donation of Constantine, in which Constantine the Great had supposedly ceded to the patriarch of Rome supreme spiritual authority and the right to

Byzantine empresses

Although often the subject of gossip and slander, the women who exercised power in Byzantium were frequently able administrators and leaders. The empress Irene, for example, who achieved dubious notoriety by ordering the blinding of her own son, was a generally competent ruler. Justinian's wife Theodora, despite a questionable past, was a skillful tactician who saved her husband's throne during the Nika rebellion. Another Theodora, mother of Michael III, was a capable regent who engineered a relatively calm return to the Iconodule position. The latter Theodora was the last empress to be chosen through a "bride show," in which eligible virgins were taken before the imperial bridegroom-to-be for his approval.

Though the wives of reigning emperors were not expected to play a significant role in affairs of state, a surprising number of imperial women found themselves in positions of great influence, typically because widows were permitted to act as regents for their sons.

The empress Zoë (below) was celebrated for her smooth complexion and fine features. Dedicating her life to beauty, she did not marry until middle age and then only for political reasons. She ended up marrying three times.

Above, a marble head, probably of the empress Theodora, wife of Justinian I. Justinian always included her name on edicts and inscriptions. Right, Theodora's monogram.

Above, a coin showing Eudocia Macrembolitissa, widow of Constantine X Ducas, with her second husband, Romanus IV, and her young son Michael VII. After the patrician Romanus was defeated at Manzikert, the bureaucratic party forced Eudocia into a convent. Irene the Hungarian (below) founded a hospital in 1136 at the Pantocrator monastery in Constantinople.

Above, Empress Eudocia, the well-educated daughter of an Athenian Sophist. Although the court was dominated by her sister-in-law Pulcheria, Eudocia wrote several poetical works, including a poem in honor of her husband, Theodosius II.

Theophilus and his wife Theodora (right) differed on the Iconoclast issue and, apparently, on other matters as well: The emperor once ordered a merchant ship belonging to Theodora burned on the grounds that an empress should not engage in business. Theophilus repaired the walls and towers of Constantinople (above) and added several halls to the main palace.

Above, a fourteenth-century interpretation of the marriage of Basil the Macedonian to Eudocia, the mistress of Michael III. Michael, seated on his throne, is talking to the bride's father while his adviser Bardas and a friend watch worriedly at right. Bardas had reason to worry, for Basil soon had him, as well as the king, murdered.

invest the emperor of the Romans. The Donation of Constantine was a forgery, but it signaled the papacy's intentions to act henceforth as a rival power to the empire.

Charlemagne was by no means the only opponent Byzantium faced during this era. Arab power was rising once again under the vigorous leadership of the Abbassid caliph Harun al-Rashid (best remembered as the caliph of the *Arabian Nights* tales), and to keep the Arabs from raiding Asia Minor, the Byzantines were forced to pay heavy tributes to Baghdad. In the Balkans, meanwhile, there arose a new king of the Bulgars—Krum. Krum's armies overran the rich grain fields of Thrace and in 813 camped outside the walls of Constantinople, burning and looting the city's suburbs. Krum's death the next year eased the Bulgar threat only temporarily.

While a succession of ineffectual or unlucky emperors tried to deal with these developments, the rivalry between pro- and anti-monkish factions continued until the death in 842 of the last Iconoclastic emperor, Theophilus the Unfortunate. Although he was associated with some notorious persecutions of Iconodules—for example, he ordered insulting verses branded on the foreheads of two well-known monks—Theophilus, too, was married to an icon venerator. Indeed, his empress Theodora was said to keep icons

in her royal bedchamber and kiss them when she thought no one was looking. It has been said that when she was seen by the court jester, who asked what she was doing, she explained that she was playing with her dolls, a remark he repeated in all innocence to the scandalized emperor.

Upon the death of Theophilus, Theodora renounced Iconoclasm in the name of her three-year-old son Michael III. This young man, who grew up to be called Michael the Drunkard, relied heavily on his advisers during his largely ineffectual reign. The most important of these advisers was Michael's uncle Bardas, who exercised power in cooperation with the patriarch Photius, one of the most learned and cosmopolitan men in Byzantine history.

The legality of Photius' elevation to the patriarchate was the subject of an involved dispute, during which Pope Nicholas I had sided against him. As a result, Photius and the pope became embroiled in a competition to see which branch of the Church would have the honor, and the ensuing advantages, of converting the kingdom of the Bulgars to Christianity. This was a quarrel that Photius and the Orthodox Church eventually won, but the interesting aspect of the situation was that it presented the spectacle of the pope negotiating with the Bulgar khan Boris in an attempt to offer him Christianity on more favorable terms. The pope was willing to allow the Bulgars to retain such practices as bathing on Wednesdays and Fridays and eating cheese during Lent.

Occasionally the Eastern and Western churches could forget their differences. Both the pope and the patriarch, for example, sponsored two apostles to the Slavs, Saints Cyril and Methodius. These remarkable brothers spread the Orthodox faith to much of east-

Cappadocian churches

The typical Byzantine monastery was not the thriving community found on Mount Athos or in Constantinople but a small gathering of ascetics eking out a bare existence and devoting most of their hours to prayer and contemplation. The ascetic life was thought to require a desolate setting, and the first monasteries had been founded in the Egyptian desert. Mindful of this example, Saint Basil, a fourth-century bishop of Caesarea, decided to settle small groups of holy men on the highland plain of Cappadocia in Asia Minor.

When work on the Cappadocian monastery began some two hundred years later, monks hollowed out the local tufa rock to form churches and chapels. The interiors of these honeycomb structures were fitted out with columns, domes, and pendentives and decorated with primitive but striking paintings. The Cappadocian churches today are a treasure trove of Byzantine art, containing fine examples of nonrepresentational Iconoclast work as well as pre- and post-Iconoclast paintings. Since the turn of this century, over one hundred and fifty chapels, churches, and monastery buildings have been identified and studied.

Right, the façade of the church of St. John the Baptist, carved from a chimneylike limestone formation. Below, frescoes of Christ and the Apostles (left) and Saint Procopius (right) from the Karanlik Kilissé, the Dark Church of the Goreme, in the Goreme valley. The church, so named because it has only one window, is the most famous of the Cappadocian rock-cut buildings.

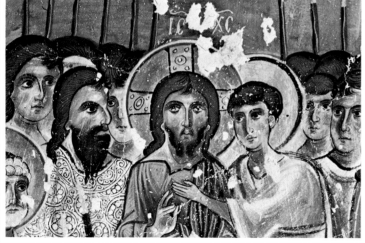

Right, a detail of the ceiling of the Sakli Kilissé, the Hidden Church of the Goreme valley. Immediately below, the entrance to the church of St. Barbara. Cappadocian churches typically have a minimum of exterior decoration. In this case, three simulated arches have been cut into the rock in imitation of a true portal.

Following pages, a surreal landscape in the Goreme valley. Inconspicuous windows and doors cut from the rock face are the only outward evidence of human habitation.

Right, the interior of the Sakli Kilissé. The columns, with mock capitals and bases, and the arches are carved to resemble true architectural elements.

Facing page, Basil I, founder of the Macedonian dynasty, as portrayed in two miniatures from the fourteenth-century chronicle of Saint John Scylitzes. Basil is shown seated on his throne (above) and with his courtiers (below). The courtiers are refusing to dine with him unless he reconciles with his son Leo, who was falsely accused of conspiring against him. Facing page, bottom right, a coin from Basil's reign. This page, right, Basil's son, after he came to the throne as Leo VI, "the Wise." Below, Leo's brother and coemperor, Alexander.

ern Europe in the ninth century. They helped to create Slavonic as a literary language and are credited with inventing the Slav's first alphabet. On one point, however, the pope and Photius disagreed: The Eastern Church maintained, in the Nicene Creed, that the Holy Spirit proceeded from the Father, the Western that it proceeded from the Father and from the Son. The Western view is called *filioquist,* because the Latin church inserted the phrase "and from the Son" *(filioque)* into the creed. "Who has ever heard of such a claim bursting from the mouth of even the most abandoned up till now?" fumed Photius in a letter circulated among the churchmen of the East. "What crooked serpent has belched his poison into their hearts. . . ?" Perhaps only another theologian can appreciate the extent of Photius' outrage. On this issue there was to be no compromise. During the last year of Michael's reign, the pope of Rome and the patriarch of Constantinople declared each other anathema, and the controversy over the correct wording of the creed remains a point of contention between Roman Catholics and the Orthodox to this day.

While Photius was engaged in these theological maneuverings, Michael III was mired in private scandal and intrigue. With Bardas running the empire, Michael was spending more and more of his time in the company of an illiterate wrestler, Basil the Macedonian. Basil first became the master of the emperor's stables and later, at Michael's request, married the imperial mistress, Eudocia Ingerina. Eventually, he persuaded Michael to elevate him to the office of coemperor. But even this was not enough.

"The Weasel"

Robert Guiscard, known as "the Weasel" or "the Wily," was one of history's most successful soldiers of fortune. His family, the Hautevilles, was Norman, descended from Scandinavian raiders who had adopted the French language and the Christian faith. Guiscard's career as a duke began when the pope granted him the territories of Apulia, Calabria, and Sicily—on the condition that he take them from their Byzantine and Arab rulers. In 1071, Guiscard captured Bari, the last outpost of Byzantine power in Italy, and a year later took Palermo, the capital of Sicily.

Though the Norman kings of Sicily depended on northern European immigrants for support, they modeled their state after Byzantium, whose riches they coveted. King Roger II went so far as to base his laws on the code of Justinian and to sign decrees with Greek inscriptions and the imperial symbol of the golden bull. In the end, the Normans became mired in the struggle between the pope and the Holy Roman emperor for control of Italy, and their kingdom fell. While it lasted, however, the kingdom of Sicily served as a unique meeting ground for Latin, Byzantine, and Moslem cultures.

Above, the Norman Robert Guiscard receiving papal investiture in 1059 as duke of Apulia, Calabria, and Sicily—lands he had yet to conquer. Sicily, an Arab province, had been dominated by Byzantium from 535 to 831. Below left, a Byzantine tombstone found at Palermo, Sicily.

Immediately below, King Roger II of Sicily, a nephew of Robert Guiscard, being crowned by Christ. The mosaic is from the church of the Martorana in Palermo.

Above, the Norman palace in Palermo. Under Roger II, who copied Byzantine rituals and symbolism, the capital of Sicily became a mecca for Greek, Arab, and European scholars. This Norman coin (center left) and precious cross (right)—the latter a gift of Pope Gregory VII—are preserved in the museum of the cathedral of Salerno, the city where Robert Guiscard made his headquarters.

Below, a silk coronation mantle woven for Roger II in 1133–1134 and later inherited by his grandson, the Holy Roman emperor Frederick II. Produced in the state-owned silk factory—another institution in the Byzantine tradition—the mantle bears an Arabic inscription in Kufic lettering and the date in Arab reckoning: A.H. 528 (year of the Hegira). It is preserved today in the Kunsthistorisches Museum, Vienna.

Country life

The glories of Byzantium were paid for in large part by onerous taxes on the rural poor. Often the tax burden was so heavy that free peasants were forced to transfer their land to owners of large estates, thus becoming tenants on farms they had formerly owned. Despite periodic attempts at reform, the situation of the free farmer was precarious at best, and the projects undertaken by an ambitious or spendthrift emperor could easily spell ruin for the farmer.

When it came to leisure activities, there is evidence that country pursuits were enjoyed with gusto. Hunting and fishing were open to all classes, and countryfolk celebrated both secular and religious festivals. Town dwellers enjoyed cabaret-style theater. The futile attempts of strict churchmen to prohibit such entertainments on Saturdays and Sundays suggest that leisure did not always give way to the demands of piety.

Raising and training falcons (right) and protecting sheep from wolves (below) are two activities of rural life illustrated in an eleventh-century codex.

An illustration from the "Appiano" codex (above) shows a man at the plow. Farming implements had improved little since ancient times. Draft animals (from a codex known as the "Chain of Job," below) were the wealth of the free peasant. Two mosaics from the imperial palace show a child herding geese (left) and a peasant bound for market (below left).

Above, a well-preserved façade from the ruins of the Great Palace, Constantinople. The palace was not a single structure but a complex of separate buildings joined by courtyards and pavilions. Many changes and additions were made over the years. Left, a scene connected with an epidemic of bovine plague that broke out during the reign of Romanus I.

Basil conspired in the murder of Bardas, and then arranged to have his benefactor Michael assassinated by a gang of street toughs, finally taking the throne himself in 867.

A more unpromising beginning for a reign can hardly be imagined, yet Basil and his descendants were to rule for 189 years, presiding over the empire at the height of its mature prosperity and splendor. As the eleventh-century historian Michael Psellus wrote, "I doubt if any other family has ever been so much favored by God as theirs has been: which is odd, when you come to think of the unlawful manner of its establishment."

Odder still, Basil's son and grandson were noted for their gentle temperaments and scholarly interests. The son, Leo the Wise, was a likable and retiring man who devoted himself to writing homilies and sermons, as well as a code that became the legal foundation of the Byzantine Empire. Unfortunately, he had to marry a total of four times to beget a male heir. To have four wives, even serially, was forbidden by the Church, and consequently Leo's reign was marred by controversy. He was finally rewarded for his troubles—his son became Constantine VII in 912.

In contrast to Leo the Wise, who was no more than a dilettante, Constantine VII was a patron of the arts,

Above right, a coin of Constantine VII and his son Romanus II. Romanus, who was said to have been more interested in food than in politics, died suddenly after a brief reign. His wife Theophano was believed to have poisoned him so that she could seduce and then marry the brilliant but ascetic general Nicephorus Phocas (depicted below, in an illustration from an eleventh-century Byzantine codex). Theophano may not have been guilty of the crimes attributed to her; however, with or without her help, Nicephorus was later assassinated in his bedroom by a band of conspirators.

a music lover, and one of the most important scholars and writers of his day. He presided over a revival of learning that had begun soon after the end of the Iconoclast period, when Michael III's uncle Bardas had reopened the university at Constantinople, and Photius and John the Grammarian, his contemporary, had influenced a whole generation of scholars. It must be said, however, that the Iconoclastic quarrel did little to relieve the arid character of Byzantine scholarship. One limiting factor that had gone unchanged was the tendency of the state to look upon the university as a training ground for bureaucrats and to think of knowledge as one more government monopoly. It is said that in the ninth century, when the caliph of Baghdad invited Leo the Mathematician to teach in his capital, the emperor Theophilus forbade him to go, feeling, in the words of one contemporary, "as if [learning] were a secret to be guarded, like the manufacture of Greek fire." With this attitude prevailing, it is hardly surprising that Byzantium produced few theoretical scientists and few authors whose works of imaginative literature have survived to be enjoyed through the ages. Digests, critiques, and histories were more to the Byzantine taste. Of these, the works of Constantine VII are still among the more informative. One of his projects was the production of a series of manuals setting forth details of court ceremonies, agricultural practices, hagiography, and a variety of other subjects—all invaluable to future students of the empire.

What Byzantine students lacked in originality they more than made up for in their passion for preserving the heritage of the classical past. Every educated Byzantine could quote Homer, and the scholar Michael Psellus was reputed to have known whole books of the *Iliad* by heart. Literacy was the rule among upper-class citizens, and women, although they were usually taught at home, were often impressively learned.

During the Macedonian era, classical themes also became more popular in the visual arts. In the illustrations of the ninth-century Paris psalter, for example, David the Psalmist is represented as an Orpheus figure, surrounded by landscapes and buildings that all bear the hallmarks of the Hellenistic style. Study of the classical philosophers was at first considered somewhat more daring. Justinian the Great had closed the Academy at Athens, and interest in Plato did not really revive until the time of Michael Psellus. Psellus' pupil John Italus taught Aristotle's views and even contended that philosophy could be studied and debated apart from theology; this was still too much for Constantinople to accept, however, and in 1088 Italus was forced to make a public recantation in Hagia Sophia. Despite this lingering suspicion of secular philosophy, Byzantine scholarship had changed greatly since the time of the Iconoclasts, when many educated people migrated to Italy to escape persecu-

tion and the stultifying intellectual climate. Not long after the end of the Macedonian era, Psellus could boast that his students included Arabs, Ethiopians, and Celts, among others.

While the seeds of cultural revival were growing, the Macedonian dynasty undertook an ambitious program of reconquest, restoring to the empire much territory that had been lost over the past centuries. The most energetic soldier-emperors of this period were, oddly enough, not even members of the imperial family. The first, Romanus Lecapenus, was the father-in-law of Constantine VII. Having elevated himself to the status of coemperor while Constantine

Ivory caskets, for both home and church use, were among the proudest creations of Byzantine craftsmen. The sacrifice of Iphigenia (upper left) is a detail from the tenth-century Veroli casket. The rosette (immediately above), a favorite motif of the ninth and tenth centuries, dominates the design of this fine casket (right). Such caskets with mythological themes were sometimes used to store bridal gifts. Far right, a ring of dancers, arms joined, circling a group of musicians in an illustration from the eleventh-century "Canticle of Moses" codex.

was still a boy, Romanus ran the empire while Constantine studied. Under his direction, Byzantium concluded a peace treaty with Simeon of Bulgaria and began an aggressive campaign in the East.

When Constantine VII's son, Romanus II, died at age twenty-four—possibly poisoned—his young widow Theophano married another general, Nicephorus Phocas, known as the "white death of the Saracens." Nicephorus II, as he was eventually called, had made his reputation when he recaptured the island of Crete in 961, destroying a stronghold of the Saracen pirates who had long menaced Byzantine shipping in the Mediterranean. As emperor, he captured Tarsus, the

city that had served as the launching point of Saracen incursions into Asia Minor, and he began an advance into Asia that culminated in the reconquest of Antioch in 969. These victories seemed to indicate that Byzantium's enemies were weakening and that a return to the glorious days of Augustus and Justinian was at hand. But it was not to be.

Unfortunately, Nicephorus Phocas was at first taken in by this illusion. When the pacified Bulgars sent an embassy to his court to demand a payment that had been guaranteed to them as part of a marriage contract, Nicephorus dismissed them angrily. "Have we Romans sunk so low that we have to pay tribute to this hideous race of beggars?" he replied. Planning to teach the Bulgars a lesson, he invited the Russian prince Svyatoslav to raid Bulgar territory. The move was solidly in the Byzantine tradition of playing off one set of barbarians against another. But this time, the strategy backfired. Svyatoslav, it turned out, had no intention of returning home after only a few raids; soon, the Balkans were in turmoil, and the Russians were overrunning Byzantine as well as Bulgar territory.

Nicephorus' arrogance also caused trouble at home. His wars were expensive, and all segments of society, even the Church, were ruthlessly taxed. Nicephorus seemed to have forgotten that, despite his promise to respect the rights of Theophano's sons by Romanus, he was basically a usurper. The fact was

Isaac I Comnenus (near right) was an Anatolian general who joined with the patriarch of Constantinople and a leader of the civil aristocracy to overthrow Michael VI in 1057. The coalition did not last, and Isaac soon retired to a monastery. Nicephorus III Botaniates (above) rebelled against Michael VII in 1078 but could do nothing to stem the advance of the Seljuk Turks in Asia Minor. Soon, only a few fortresses, like this one (far right) at Kutahya on the Porusk River, remained in Byzantine hands.

not lost on others, however, and at the end of A.D. 969, Nicephorus was murdered in his bedchamber by a band of conspirators led by John Tzimisces, who assumed the throne as John I and managed to force Svyatoslav back to Kiev. Nevertheless, the specter of a Russian fleet descending on the Bosporus had made its impression on Constantinople. It was a fear that would be revived periodically and is still alive today.

Although Nicephorus Phocas ruled for only six years, his career illustrates a much more gradual development. Ever so slowly, Byzantium was being transformed from a Roman imperial state, distin-

guished by a centralized bureaucracy and a citizen army, into a feudalistic society. As emperor, Nicephorus recognized that his interests lay in halting this trend, yet his own background and inclinations are evidence of just how difficult a reversal of the process would have been.

Toward the rise of the monasteries, for example, Nicephorus' attitude was ambivalent. As emperor, he issued an edict severely curtailing the passage of private property into monastic hands. Criticizing the disease of greed which had infected so many religious communities, Nicephorus observed bitterly that the Apostles could hardly have intended for their succes-

sors to become the masters of large estates. Yet, despite the bitter tone of his edict, Nicephorus himself had ascetic tendencies. He wore a hair shirt next to his skin, and he corresponded with the founders of the Grand Lavra, the first large monastic community, on Mount Athos. The monks there, who blamed the seductive influence of Theophano for Nicephorus' antimonastic policies, maintain to this day that the soldier-emperor intended to retire from public life to end his days in a monastic cell.

In any case, the decrees of Nicephorus did not halt the growth of Mount Athos. By the time of John Tzimisces, there were some fifty-eight communities and an estimated three thousand monks. The peninsula, which for centuries had been home to a few hermits and scattered bands of disciples, now grew rapidly into a semiautonomous republic of monks so self-contained in its prosperity that the fall of the empire centuries later scarcely affected it at all.

In addition to the problem of monasticism, Nicephorus was forced to deal with the growing concentration of land in the hands of a few powerful families. The Phocas family was itself among the most prominent of these landlords, and in the end Nicephorus did not go against his own interests and those of his class. He did proclaim a law raising the amount

Bulgaria's domain

In the year 813, when the Bulgar khan Krum failed in his attempt to take Constantinople, he vented his frustration by burning churches in the suburbs of the capital and making human sacrifices outside the Golden Door. By the end of the ninth century, however, the fearsome Bulgars had adopted Slavic culture and embraced Orthodox Christianity. Several decades later, the Bulgar leader Simeon was able to style himself czar, or emperor, and to claim domains that stretched from the Adriatic to the gates of Constantinople.

The costs of civilization were high. Bulgaria soon found itself in the position of a buffer state between the Byzantines, who regarded the Bulgars as barbarians, and advancing waves of Magyars, Turkic Pechenegs, and Russians. At home, the strains of adapting to new ways led to the rise of the Bogomil heresy. Regarding the world and all its works as the creations of Satan, these heretics preached passive resistance against church and state.

Decisively defeated by Basil II in 1018, the Bulgarian state was absorbed into the Byzantine Empire and did not re-emerge until Constantinople fell into the hands of the Latin Crusaders.

Above, Constantine Asen and his wife, in a fresco executed during their reign, ca. 1259. Right, a mounted warrior drags a captive by the hair. This detail from a proto-Bulgar gold ewer is one of the earliest depictions of a soldier in chain-mail armor. The ewer, part of a remarkable gold treasure accidentally discovered in 1799, shows Sassanid Persian as well as Byzantine influence.

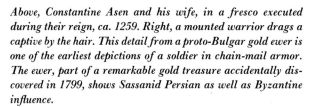

Above, the remains of a royal Bulgarian palace at Zarevir, Bulgaria. Right, the Bulgar leader Simeon leading a rout of the Byzantine army.

Above, King Kaloyan of Bulgaria in a fresco from the church of Bojana, offering a model of the church to God. In imitation of Basil II, "the Bulgar-slayer," Kaloyan called himself "the Roman-slayer" and attacked the Latin empire of Constantinople in 1205. The Latins never really recovered from this assault. Below, the Yantra River near Trnovo, which was the ancient capital of the Bulgars, in northern Bulgaria.

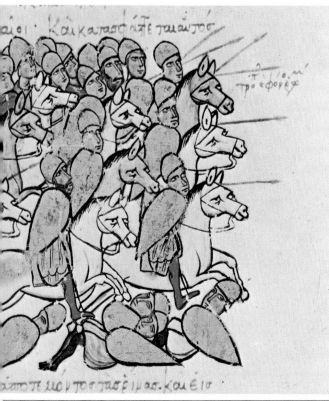

of territory necessary for a peasant to qualify as a citizen-soldier, but the effect of the law was to downgrade the poorer militiamen to the status of ordinary peasants while the richer officers became petty squires. A similar process was taking place among the wealthier landowners, whose family traditions were also those of military service. As the historian J. B. Bury wrote, the knights of Anatolia often "possessed large domains and resembled feudal barons rather than Roman officers."

The last emperor strong enough to keep these feudal forces in check was the son of the much maligned Theophano and a namesake of the founder of the dynasty—Basil. A soldier through and through, Basil II had little use for the affected, euphuistic rhetoric of Constantinople's bureaucrats. Yet, he was even more opposed to the landowners. He relieved the tax burden that had fallen on the shoulders of the poor farmers of the empire, and he decreed that large landlords would have to document their titles to their domains. In the case of some properties that had originally belonged to the imperial crown, landowners were requested to demonstrate a title dating back a minimum of a thousand years.

Basil deserves to be remembered as a land reformer, but he is far better known as a warrior. After

The accession of Alexius Comnenus (left) in 1081 marked the final victory of the feudal aristocrats over the bureaucratic party. Below, Saint Mark, one of eighty miniature enamel figures that decorate the Pala d'Oro, a gold altarpiece in the Byzantine tradition, now in St. Mark's Cathedral, Venice. The cathedral itself was inspired by the now vanished church of the Holy Apostles in Constantinople.

centuries of trouble in the Balkans, it was his task to defeat the Bulgars permanently and place the region firmly under Byzantine rule. Nicknamed the "Bulgar-slayer," Basil struck terror into the hearts of his enemies by his treatment of some fourteen thousand Bulgar prisoners captured in 1014. Blinding ninety-nine out of every hundred men, he sent the prisoners back home in the care of the one percent who could still see. The spectacle of this army of cripples was so pitiful that the Bulgar king Samuel, who had ridden out to welcome the prisoners in ignorance of their fate, suffered a stroke and died within weeks.

As totally dedicated as Basil was to protecting the empire, there was one thing that he absolutely would not do for the benefit of the crown—marry. He did have a plan to wed his niece Zoë to the Holy Roman emperor Otto III, but this union, which would have united the Eastern and Western empires under a single house, fell through, because of Otto's death. As a result, when the bachelor emperor died in his seventies, he left as heirs only his sixty-five-year-old brother Constantine VIII and three unmarried nieces.

The hopes of the Macedonian line now devolved upon Zoë. Forty-seven years old when her uncle died,

she had no prospect of ever bearing an heir. Yet, she was immensely popular with the people of Constantinople and was the last chance of the bureaucratic party. The aged Constantine, totally unable to control the rebellious landlords, urged her to marry, and the choice fell on the administrator of Constantinople, Romanus Argyrus. Romanus, who was forced on pain of execution to divorce his beloved wife of many years, apparently had no taste for the honor that had come his way and, once installed as emperor, began to neglect Zoë. This was a mistake. A vain woman who looked and felt much younger than her

An illustration from a thirteenth-century codex (immediately below) shows an emperor receiving ambassadors from the East. Bottom, from the same codex, Byzantine ships using brass tubes to shoot Greek fire at an enemy galley.

tione diuina sca Eusta xpianozum.

N e donc ne aub auant ne puis.

Ant ces deus nes sentrecoisent
Et li uno daus les autres uirent
Ne sorent dire ne pnser

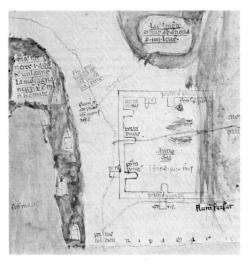

Above, the Crusaders' departure for the Holy Land. Travel by sea (far left) avoided the Balkans and Asia Minor and was preferred by those who could afford it. Near left, a map of Antioch, the city captured by Alexius I's enemy Bohemund in 1098. Bottom left, the construction of a Venetian ship. Leaders of the Fourth Crusade chartered Venetian vessels for their transport to Jerusalem.

years, Zoë soon became enamored of a handsome young man named Michael, the brother of a powerful court eunuch, John the Orphanotrophus. Not long after, Romanus was found mysteriously murdered in his bath, and Zoë married Michael.

Her life was far from peaceful, however, for Michael died suddenly, and John was unwilling to give up his influence. Only when John became too sure of himself and tried to have Zoë put away in a convent did his plans fall apart. With the crowds in the streets screaming their support for Zoë, rebels captured John and brought Zoë back in triumph. Finally, in her mid-sixties, she married a third time, choosing another bureaucrat, Constantine Monomachus.

Byzantium had managed to weather periods of intrigue and incompetence in the past, but now the greed of the landowners and the moral bankruptcy of the court and bureaucracy combined to do irrepara-

Above, the Crusaders' assault on Constantinople, from a mosaic in the church of San Giovanni, Ravenna. Following pages, a sixteenth-century view of Galata, the town across the Golden Horn from Constantinople that became a Genoese colony as a result of Genoa's alliance with Michael Paleologus.

ble damage. Constantine Monomachus has the distinction of being the first ruler in Byzantine history to devalue the currency—a step that many historians consider to be the most important single event in precipitating the empire's decline. Two other events in the succeeding decades sealed Byzantium's fate. One was the final schism between Rome and Constantinople, which occurred in 1054, when the Roman cardinal Humbert marched into Hagia Sophia and revealed a document excommunicating the patriarch of Constantinople. The other was a disastrous battle in 1071 at Manzikert in Asia Minor, in

Above, the emperors of the Paleologue dynasty, which ruled from 1261 to 1453, as portrayed in a Byzantine codex. The Paleologue emperors—with the exception of Michael VIII, who founded the dynasty—were mediocrities, more interested in court intrigue than in the defense of the empire.

which the Seljuk Turkish sultan Alp Arslan turned back a huge but totally disorganized Byzantine army.

After a decade of near anarchy, the seizure of the throne by Alexius Comnenus in 1081 marked the final victory of the feudal party. The economic and military bases of the empire were by now badly eroded, and the superstructure of administration, church, and schools was tottering on its foundations. Yet to all outward appearances, the empire remained impressive. In this compromised condition, Byzantium was now destined to be pushed into closer and closer contact with the rising states of western

Europe. At first, Western Christendom would be dazzled by the splendor of its venerable neighbor. But it was inevitable that when the West finally grew disillusioned, its awe would turn to contempt and, eventually, to opportunism.

Alexius Comnenus was an astute man who saw clearly the dangerous position of the empire and was prepared to take drastic measures to shore it up. During his reign, Byzantium was menaced by a number of enemies: a tribe known as the Pechenegs from beyond the Danube; the Bogomil heretics, who preached that the world and all its creatures were the work of the devil; and most important, the Normans, who had carved out a kingdom in Sicily. Alexius held them all at bay, but in dealing with the Normans he was forced to make an alliance with Venice. Bargaining for the assistance of the Venetian fleet, Alexius guaranteed the city's merchants special privileges which gave them a competitive advantage over the merchants of Constantinople. In effect, he had handed over to the island republic of Venice the leadership in Mediterranean commerce.

The Venetian treaty was a hard bargain but one that at least served its purpose. Alexius' next move had a less satisfactory outcome. Seeing that the Seljuk Turks had been left vulnerable by the death of the sultan Malik Shah in 1092, Alexius decided that the time was ripe for an aggressive strike. In anticipation of such a campaign, he appealed for help from the West. What Alexius had in mind was a few detachments of mercenaries willing to fight under his banner in Asia Minor. What he got was something quite different: the Crusaders, a multitude, unarmed and untrained for the most part, that descended on his domains like a plague of locusts.

Translated by ambitious Pope Urban II into a request for a holy war, Alexius' modest appeal had touched off the First Crusade. In fact, the first wave of Crusaders to reach Byzantine territory was not an army at all but a rabble of vagrants, peasants, and poor knights led by the itinerant preacher Peter the Hermit. From his palace in Constantinople, Alexius listened in horror to reports of their progress across the countryside, where they ravaged crops, stole, and murdered indiscriminately. Determined to save his capital, Alexius resorted to a desperate strategy. Urging the marchers to make their way to Jerusalem as quickly as possible, he arranged for boats to ship them across the Bosporus—straight into the hands of the Turks, who promptly massacred them.

The second wave of Crusaders was not so easily disposed of. This was the true army, and among the leaders was an old enemy of Alexius'—Bohemund, son of the Norman Robert Guiscard. Alexius' daughter

Above and right, the church of Hagia Sophia in Trebizond, on the Black Sea. When Constantinople fell to the Crusaders in 1204, two nephews of the emperor Andronicus Comnenus sought refuge in Trebizond and made the city the capital of their exiled state. Later, Trebizond survived the fall of Byzantium and remained independent until 1461. Below, a monumental gate, the remains of a late Roman construction on the road between Constantinople and Nicaea.

Legacy of Byzantium

The influence of Byzantium on the developing cultures of the Arab world and western Europe was incalculable though often unappreciated by the beneficiaries. Contacts with the Byzantines from Justinian's time on helped set the stage for the Italian Renaissance. During the fifteenth century, Greek scholars played an especially important role in reviving interest in classical studies.

The labors of Byzantium's missionaries and artists had more immediate results. Missionaries spread their faith throughout the Balkans, Russia, and Armenia, and it was the Greek brothers Cyril and Methodius who gave the Slavs their first alphabet. Among the most influential contributions of Byzantine artists were the traditional Orthodox five-domed church and the icon. To Byzantium's artists can also be attributed the development of mosaics, whose golden tessarae so infused churches with a spiritual glow that it was sometimes said that the master mosaicists practiced the "art of light." Remarkably, Byzantine art and culture continued to evolve and exert influence for hundreds of years after the fall of the Eastern Empire.

Byzantine churches reflect the empire's vast domains, geographically distant but culturally unified: the Cattolica di Stilo (above left), an example of middle Byzantine architecture, in Calabria; a fresco from the monastery of St. Catherine in the Sinai (immediately above); the church of Sveti Skolevi, in Mtzsheta, ancient capital of Georgia (left); the thirteenth-to-fourteenth-century monastery of Gračanica, Serbia (below left); and the early Byzantine basilica of San Vitale, Ravenna (immediately below).

Facing page, the tenth-century church of the Holy Cross in Armenia (top right); the church of Apentiko in Mistra in the Peloponnesus (center right); a dramatic cliffside church in the rocky Meteora valley of Thessaly (bottom right); and the church of Hosios Lukas in Phocia (bottom left).

Convent of St. Therapon

Novgorod
Vladimir
Pskov

Kiev

Suceava
Moldavia

Aquileia
Venice
Gračanica
Belgrade
Ravenna
Studenica
Trnovo
Sopocani
Bojana
Rome
Ohrid
Thessalonica
Kastoria
Meteora
Arta
Rossano
Daphne
Ephesus
Palermo
Stilo
Athens
Tralles
Mistra

BLACK SEA

Tiflis

Sinope
Trebizond

Lake Sevan
Mtzsheta
Byzantium
Nicaea
Akhtamar
Caesarea
Nazianzus
Edessa
Alanya
Dura Europos
Palmyra

Cyprus

Crete

MEDITERRANEAN SEA

Jerusalem

Sinai
St. Catharine

Anna Comnena has left us a vivid description of the contempt and suspicion Byzantium felt for these holy warriors who insisted on addressing Alexius by the insulting title of King of the Greeks (to be dismissed as merely Greek was an affront, for the Byzantines considered themselves heirs of ancient Rome). Such an upheaval, uprooting thousands of Christians in the name of the faith, had never before occurred within human memory. The simpler-minded were urged on by the real desire of worshiping at Christ's sepulcher and visiting the sacred places, but the more astute had another secret reason—namely, the hope that while on their travels they might be able to find a pretext for seeing the capital itself.

Due to the well-considered policy of Alexius, no such pretext appeared—at least not on this particular Crusade. As emperor of the Romans, Alexius demanded that the leaders of the Crusaders, including Godfrey of Bouillon, swear allegiance to him. When Godfrey refused, the food supply to his army was promptly cut off. In the end, Godfrey grudgingly complied, and the Crusaders helped the Byzantines recapture Turkish territory in Asia Minor before pushing on to Jerusalem, where their assault on the Holy Land was aided by only a token Byzantine force. Both western "Latins" and eastern "Romans" had considerable success in gaining their military ob-

The church of the Savior in Chora (above) exemplifies the art of the Paleologue revival. Facing page, Theodore Metochites, founder and patron of the church, presenting a gift to Christ (above left); the prophet Zacharias (above right); and a detail from the mosaic The Virgin Blessed by the Priests *(below). Following pages, Rumeli Hisari, or "The European Fortress," erected by Sultan Mohammed II on the shores of the Bosporus in 1452.*

jectives, but the legacy of the First Crusade was one of bitterness. With direct trade between Syria and western Europe now possible and Venetian merchants now doing business within the walls of Constantinople itself, Byzantium was losing its grip on the flow of international commerce. In addition, the Crusaders felt that the emperor had called them to take up the Cross only to betray them at the last minute; they refused to believe that Constantinople had not wanted a Crusade in the first place. The practical attitude Byzantium had been forced to adopt in its centuries-long defense of Europe from the threat of Islam—that of fighting to gain military control of areas without dwelling heavily on ideological, moralistic justification—had earned it no gratitude.

Although Alexius' cautious policies were continued by his son John II, his g a sor Manuel Comnenus

was less realistic. A courageous and brilliant man, Manuel let himself be deceived into believing that the empire was as vigorous as he was. Manuel married twice, both times to Western princesses, and his son and heir, another Alexius, was wed to Agnes, the seven-year-old daughter of Louis VII of France. In contrast to his predecessors, Manuel admired some aspects of Western culture, and during his reign the customs of chivalry made their appearance within the imperial court. Manuel himself participated in jousting tournaments, much to the dismay of the more conservative citizens of his capital. He also meddled in the politics of the continent. His original hopes for

an alliance with Conrad III of Germany were frustrated by the poorly organized Second Crusade, and after Conrad's death, Manuel became locked in a rivalry with Conrad's successor, Frederick Barbarossa, for control of Italy.

While Manuel was dreaming of restoring his true position as universal emperor, the situation at home was steadily deteriorating. By the time Manuel died, anti-Western feeling was so strong that his cousin Andronicus was soon able to depose the young heir to the throne. Already elderly and with a reputation as a profligate and adventurer, Andronicus tried to control the feudal families and stamp out rampant corruption. His aims—including relief for the peasants and the expulsion of Venetian traders from Constantinople—were more popular than his methods. Unable to make progress by any other means, Andronicus resorted to a reign of terror, torturing and murdering all who opposed him. Furthermore, he

Facing page, the emperor John Cantacuzene (above left), who reigned from 1347 to 1355, and the patriarch Joseph II (below left), who served from 1416. Both were advocates of a rapprochement with Rome. Facing page, right, a French view of the siege of Constantinople showing Turkish ships in the Golden Horn. A miniature, this page, from the Turkish Book of Achievements reveals the jubilation of the victorious Turks as they sack the great city.

outraged the increasingly fickle populace of the capital by canceling the Hippodrome races on the grounds that they were a luxury the empire could no longer afford. In a rebellion of 1185, Andronicus was dragged into the streets and torn to pieces by the vengeful mob.

Andronicus' successor Isaac II Angelus was a descendant of the Comnenus family on his mother's side, and he seemed to regard the empire as his personal inheritance. According to one contemporary historian, Isaac "sold offices as vegetables were sold in the market." He also reinstated the races at the Hippodrome and, in general, conducted himself as if de-

Above, John VIII Paleologus, portrayed on a medal by Pisanello that was executed during the emperor's stay in Florence for the ecumenical council of 1439. Facing page, Sultan Mohammed II, conqueror of Byzantium in 1453. This painting by Constanza da Ferrara is believed to have been done from life while the artist was a resident of Constantinople.

termined to empty the imperial treasury in one generation. Under Isaac, the empire was so weakened that when the aging Frederick Barbarossa passed through Constantinople on the Third Crusade, only his haste to reach the Holy Land before he died—a goal he did not attain—prevented him from trying to take the city.

In the end, it was a coup against Isaac that provided the pretext for conquest by Westerners that Anna Comnena had written of a century earlier. Isaac was driven from the throne by his brother in 1195, and his son, the future Alexius IV, took refuge in Germany, where he appealed to the organizers of the Fourth Crusade for help in reinstating his father to power. The Venetian doge had already persuaded the Crusaders to turn over to him the Byzantine port of Zara on the Adriatic as partial payment for their use of the Venetian fleet; now, expecting to be well paid for his efforts, he took up the cause of Alexius. The result was the famous sack of Constantinople. After fierce fighting, the Crusaders' assault on Constantinople succeeded only when the pretender had fled and the people released Isaac from prison and opened the gates. Unfortunately, neither Isaac nor his son, the new coemperor, had the money that had been promised to the Crusaders. While Alexius stalled, the Crusaders grew more and more impatient and the

aristocrats of Byzantium more outraged. Finally, another coup against Alexius and Isaac gave the Crusaders the excuse they had been looking for. Having agreed in advance how they would divide up the wealth of Romania, as they now called Byzantium, they fell to the task at hand. As their chronicler Villehardouin enthusiastically described it: "Since the world was created, never had so much booty been won in any one city!"

For nine centuries, Constantinople had defended the heritage of Greece, Rome, and early Christianity against endless waves of invaders, barbarian and Moslem alike. Now, in a matter of days, this proud city was ravaged by an army of Christians who had begun their campaign, ironically, with the avowed goal of saving the Holy Places from the infidel. Seizing Constantinople on April 13, 1204, the Crusaders pillaged for three days, robbing, raping, and taking particular delight in the torturing of Orthodox priests. Holy relics, many from the original collection of Saint Helena, were carted off to France, and precious manuscripts, many of them the only surviving copies of Greek and Roman classics, were wantonly put to the torch. Hagia Sophia, still universally acknowledged to be one of the most beautiful churches in Christendom, became the scene of the looters' drunken victory celebration. Its treasures were destroyed or stolen, and its altars were used as gaming tables. Some of the revelers even brought in a prostitute and installed her on the patriarch's throne to preside over the destruction.

When calm finally returned, Baldwin, count of Flanders, was in power, styling himself the "new Augustus." At the time, the richest territory of the empire—including the best ports and nearly half the capital—was under the control of Venice. Byzantium seemed to be finished, yet only fifty-seven years later a new dynasty was to rise like a phoenix from the ashes of the plundered empire. Soon after the fall of Constantinople, escaping aristocrats had set up several governments in exile: the despotate of Epirus in the northwest; the island of Rhodes; the so-called empire of Trebizond on the Black Sea; and the domains of the Lascarid family at Nicaea. The last of these gradually emerged as the most powerful, and under Michael Paleologus, a cousin of the last Lascarid pretender, the family managed to wrest Constantinople from the hands of the hated Latins. Michael's plan for retaking Constantinople had been based on an alliance with Venice's rival Genoa. But only days after a costly treaty with the Genoese was signed, one of Michael's generals, who had been reconnoitering in the vicinity, discovered almost by accident that the

Venetian fleet had sailed out of the Golden Horn. With scarcely a blow struck, he marched his army into Constantinople, and for the Byzantines, the city became once again, as Michael Paleologus proclaimed it, "the acropolis of the Universe."

The resurrected empire was a frail thing indeed. Commanding few soldiers and possessing little money, the rulers were forced to seek aid in the West. In return for this aid, which did not amount to much in any case, they were forced to acknowledge the supremacy of the pope—a policy that aroused deep resentment at home. In 1347, the Black Death carried off at least a quarter of the empire's population; in the same year, a new emperor, John VI, was reduced to using a coronation diadem with glass jewels, the real ones having been sold off. Finally, in 1400, the emperor was forced to undertake a melancholy pilgrimage to the courts of Charles VI of France and Henry IV of England, where his dignified bearing and impeccable white robes evoked admiration and sympathy but only token contributions to the cause of saving New Rome.

Almost unbelievably, in the midst of these deteriorating conditions, Byzantine culture exhibited a final burst of energy. Mosaics produced during this period are notable for their humanistic spirit, and portraits in particular display a depth of emotion and individualized expression unparalleled in earlier mosaic work. Intellectual life also flourished, and Byzantium's scholars, freed at last from the burden of insisting that they were Roman and not Greek, now began to use the once scorned term "Hellene" as a badge of pride. The scholar Georgius Gemistus Pletho, who shocked his religious friends by writing of God as Zeus, suggested that the state could be revived by reorganizing it along the lines of an ideal Platonic state. The Church, meanwhile, had turned increasingly to mysticism.

There was one point on which nearly all Byzantines could agree. Submission to the pope of Rome was every bit as distasteful as the prospect of falling under the sway of the Turkish sultan. The emperor John VIII finally pushed through a formal act of union with Rome by arranging for a hand-picked delegation of the more accommodating Greek bishops to represent him at a council held in Florence in 1439. A document of union was duly signed but never really accepted by the people of Constantinople. Failing to produce the hoped-for aid from the Latins, John's policy succeeded only in provoking riots and disaffection among his own subjects.

Not until May of 1453, when heavily armed Turkish troops led by Mohammed II were encamped outside the walls of the capital, did Byzantium finally forget its internal differences over the question of union with Rome. Aware that this was one siege Constantinople's fabled walls would not withstand, the citizens flocked to Hagia Sophia to hear the popular emperor, appropriately named Constantine XI, deliver a ringing exhortation, reminding them that they were the true heirs of Greece and Rome and vowing to die for the True Faith. Within twenty-four hours, Constantine had fulfilled his vow, flinging off his royal insignia to join in the street fighting as Turkish soldiers stormed the city. His body was never conclusively identified.

Western Christendom, despite so many warnings, received the news of the fall of the "God-guarded City" with surprise and horror. Yet, there was also some feeling that the Byzantines, by resisting union with the Church of Rome, had fatalistically accepted their own demise as a people. In fact, with its population and economic power for so long greatly diminished, the fall of Constantinople was virtually inevitable. But by refusing to accept the policies of their own emperors, the people of Byzantium had gallantly preserved what was for them even more important than the survival of their once great capital—the spiritual integrity of the Orthodox Church.

Not long after the conquest, the monk George Scholarius Gennadius, formerly a leader of the opposition to union, was discovered by Sultan Mohammed in the house of a rich Turk, to whom he had been sold as a slave. The sultan brought him back to Constantinople to serve as patriarch. Later sultans were less tolerant, but another center of Orthodoxy had already been established—in Russia. Here, one of the last survivors of the Paleologues had found a home and a throne. Curiously, the marriage of Zoë Paleologus to Czar Ivan III was arranged by the pope, who thought her a convert to Roman Catholicism. But the conversion of Zoë proved to be as ephemeral as the union with Rome. Once in Russia, she promptly rejoined the Orthodox Church. Her son, Vasili III, grew up far removed from the dreams of a New Rome, yet he worshiped in a faith that owed its existence to Constantine's miracle twelve centuries earlier.

The Turks

They came out of central Asia as tribal nomads, living in tents and fighting from horseback, driving their herds before them. By the sixth century A.D. they already had been given the name Tu-kueh, the Chinese word for Turks. In the eighth century, the Tu-kueh, or Turks, controlled Samarkand on the silk route to Cathay. In the ninth and tenth centuries, they worshiped Allah. Wandering ever westward they arrived on what was then the center stage of history—the Middle East—at an opportune moment: The Byzantine Empire was in decline and the empire of the Arab caliphs was fragmenting into warring kingdoms. The Turks took full advantage of the resultant vulnerability of these two empires. Picking up the banner of the Byzantines, they conquered the Arabs and eventually replaced them both.

The first Turks to achieve prominence were the Seljuks, in the eleventh century. Although they paid homage to the Arab caliph, the Seljuks ruled over Persia, Mesopotamia, and Syria—the region bordering the Byzantine Empire. In 1071, a Seljuk force defeated a Byzantine army in Armenia, and bands of Turkish nomads, warriors, and religious extremists flooded into the Byzantine territories of Asia Minor, or Anatolia. The Seljuks then established an elegant capital at Konya, in central Anatolia. A more rustic and rugged Turkish society grew up on the frontier with Byzantium, where petty warfare and pillage were perpetual. This area was the realm of the *ghazis,* "warriors of the faith." Dedicated to holy war against the infidel, the ghazis lived by booty; when the Seljuk sultans did not send them on expeditions against the Christians, they attacked and raided for Allah. At the end of the thirteenth century, ten autonomous ghazi principalities were engaged in fighting the infidel along the Byzantine border. One of them, situated near the town of Soyut, about one hundred miles southeast of Constantinople, was ruled by a brilliant chieftan called Osman, or Othman, who gave his name and his mission to a dynasty that would reign for six centuries as the Ottoman Turkish Empire.

Soyut was the ghazi district closest to Constantinople. This proximity gave Osman an advantage over the more distant chieftains: The Byzantine Greeks abandoned territory elsewhere in Anatolia but they could not afford to evacuate their frontier with Osman. As ghazi bands in the recently peaceful areas disintegrated for lack of enemies, their holy warriors flocked to Osman, who could offer them the opportunity for continual service. After he routed a Byzantine army in 1301, Osman was joined by still more fighting Turks, and even by Greek defectors. He also wel-

comed Christians who recognized his authority—and thus the supremacy of Islam—and let them worship as they pleased.

The fortified Byzantine cities of Bursa, Nicaea, and Nicomedia, in Asia Minor, remained for Osman to conquer. Wary of attacking them directly, Osman instead plundered and occupied the surrounding countryside, cutting the cities off from sustenance—and from Constantinople. Then he began a long siege of Bursa. The city fell in 1326, in time for Osman to be buried there, and Orkhan, his son, made Bursa his new capital.

A daring innovator, Orkhan reorganized Osman's volunteer horsemen into an efficient professional standing army that captured Nicaea and Nicomedia. Intervening in the Byzantine civil wars, he married a daughter of John Cantacuzene, a pretender to the Byzantine throne, and lent his new father-in-law six

The Blue Mosque of Sultan Ahmed I (preceding page) is one of the masterworks of the Ottoman Empire, which began as a rustic frontier state in Anatolia (left). Remains of Turkish fortresses in Anatolia survive at Alanya (above), Dogubayezid (below, far left), and Soyut (below), the original seat of the Ottoman holy warriors. Below left, a thirteenth-century tomb near Lake Van.

thousand troops. Cantacuzene, his ranks thus strengthened, was able to march into Constantinople and become coemperor. But it was the Ottomans who ultimately benefitted. Orkhan realized that his Byzantine in-laws could not confront their European enemies without his aid, and he quickly learned to play the European rivals against each other.

In 1352, Cantacuzene asked Orkhan to help defend Constantinople against a coalition of Venetians, Serbs, and Bulgarians, promising him in return a fortress near Gallipoli, on the European side of the Dardanelles. The Ottomans obliged, but they appropriated Gallipoli as well as the promised fortress. Moreover, Orkhan sent Turkish nomads to settle on the European side and raided deeper into Byzantine lands. Cantacuzene could only protest, for the Ottomans had nearly surrounded Constantinople and the emperor was becoming little more than Orkhan's vassal. The Turks were in Europe to stay.

Orkhan's Balkan campaign was led by his first son, Suleiman, who died in 1358. When Orkhan died in

1359, he was succeeded by his second son, who became Sultan Murad I. Murad combined shrewd statesmanship with military brilliance—and brutality. Capturing Chorlu, which was located approximately halfway between Adrianople and Constantinople, he ordered the garrison massacred and its commander decapitated. This so terrified the Thracians that they surrendered the fortified city of Adrianople without a fight, giving the Turks command of the main highway between Constantinople and the West. Murad made Adrianople the new Ottoman capital and built palaces and mosques in the city. The message he conveyed was clear: Submit and prosper, or resist and die.

Resistance was difficult. Demoralized by the Black Death, which had killed at least one quarter of the population of Europe, and torn by their own religious and economic rivalries, the Christian kingdoms could unite only rarely against the Ottoman threat. After a coalition of Serbia, Hungary, Bosnia, and other states was defeated on the Maritza River in 1363, it would

Osman I (left) founded the dynasty that bears his name. (In Arabic it is Othman, from which comes Ottoman.) As each new sultan ascended the throne, he was invested with Osman's sword, the symbol of the dynasty, while a holy man intoned, "May he be as good as Osman." Osman died in 1326 as his warriors were capturing Bursa. The city became the first Ottoman capital and a center of art, learning, and theology. Osman and all the early sultans are buried there. Above right, the mausoleum of Bursa's Green Mosque, containing the elaborately tiled tomb of Mohammed I (below right).

On assuming the throne after the death of Osman, Orkhan (above) was proclaimed "Sultan, son of the Sultan of the Ghazis, Ghazi son of Ghazi, Marquis of the Hero of the World." Although he was the younger of Osman's two sons, his father had picked him to rule because of his warlike spirit. His scholarly brother declined Orkhan's offer to share their inheritance and instead served Orkhan as vizier. Brothers of later sultans were not so fortunate.

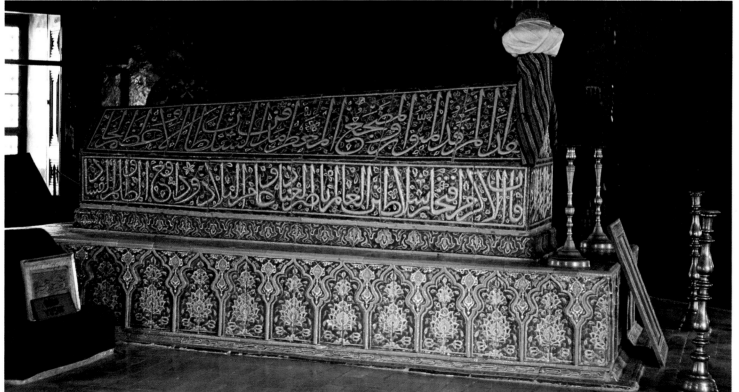

Ruthless to his enemies, Murad I (left) was a skilled and just administrator whose rule brought peace and order to the conquered European territories. In 1362, he took the ancient city of Adrianople and made it his capital. Among the fine mosques the sultans gave the city is the mosque of Selim II (below), built in 1575 by Sinan, probably the greatest Ottoman architect, and the Three Balconied Mosque of Murad II (right) which dates from 1434.

be twenty years before the Europeans could gather their forces again.

Makeshift alliances of mistrustful rivals were no match for the efficient, well-drilled Ottoman army and its elite corps of *janissaries* (new troops). These captive Christian youths, who were forcibly converted to Islam, underwent rigorous training for warfare. As the sultan's personal slaves, janissaries were forbidden to marry, own property, or take up any occupation other than fighting. Lacking heirs and kept in relative luxury, isolated from other elements of Ottoman society, their unquestioning obedience to their sultan—and to each other—was almost assured.

Discipline and loyalty were of supreme importance to Murad. In the lull after his Maritsa victory, he organized several programs aimed at unifying his polyglot empire and spreading Islamic values and customs. To this end, Turks from Anatolia were brought in to settle the Balkans; the *sepahis* (cavalrymen) were granted tax-free fiefs in conquered territory; and Moslem farmers tilled the soil and served in the militia, which was called up in time of war. Some Christians were required to pay a head tax in place of military service but many converted instead. The Greek-Orthodox Bulgarians, who had been persecuted by the Catholic Hungarians, welcomed the religious tolerance under Ottoman rule, and their

prince donated a daughter to Murad's harem.

Under Murad's rule, Prince Lazar of Serbia was reduced to vassalage and Serbian troops fought alongside the Turks in Anatolia. When some of the Serbian auxiliaries were executed for insubordination, Lazar rebelled, and Ottoman vassals throughout the Balkans rallied around him with a force of one hundred thousand assorted central European troops. Murad himself led the Ottoman army to meet the insurgents at Kosovo, in Serbia, on August 27, 1389, with his sons Bayezid and Yakub commanding the flanks. During the battle, one of Lazar's allies, a son-in-law who may have sold out to Murad, deserted. Amidst the ensuing confusion, the Ottoman cavalry routed the ranks of the Christians, and Prince Lazar was taken captive.

The rebellion was over—but so was Murad's reign. A Serbian nobleman had pretended to desert to Murad during the battle, and when escorted to the sultan's tent in feigned submission he plunged a dagger into Murad's breast. The last act of the dying

Caravansaries

To protect and encourage the commerce of the empire, the Ottoman sultans built hundreds of caravansaries throughout their domains. Essentially overnight hostels for merchants transporting their goods, the caravansaries were located one day's journey from each other along the well-maintained roads, and at bridges and towns. Many could also be used as bazaars, and new towns and commercial centers often sprang up around them. Sultans and wealthy officials supported caravansaries, which offered free food and lodging for three days to all travelers, regardless of rank or status. One great caravansary contained two hundred rooms and a courtyard big enough for five thousand horses. At sundown each guest received a bowl of soup, a loaf of bread, and a candle, and each horse was fed a bag of oats. Following the evening prayer, the house band played and the gates swung shut. In the morning, before the innkeeper was allowed to open the gates, he had to ask his guests whether they had all their possessions; if he neglected to do this he was required to make restitution for any losses. In 1555, the ambassador of the Holy Roman emperor noted that "even pashas when they travel make use of the caravansaries. . . . I thought myself lodged as well as in the palace of a prince."

The caravansary, as can be seen from the ruins of Rubat-Sharaf near the Iranian border (left) and from a miniature of the period (right), was constructed as a hollow square with rooms and eating platforms that surrounded a great courtyard in which the travelers, horses, camels, mules, and wagons were kept. Armed guards were always on duty, and when the gate such as the one at Kirşehir (center right) was shut, the caravansary was secure against bandits. Below, evening in a caravansary, as depicted in an old miniature. Note the chain across the guarded gate and the innkeeper on his white horse. The Ottomans were not the first to invest heavily in these inns: The Sultan Han, with its magnificent vaulted ceilings (bottom right), dates from Seljuk times.

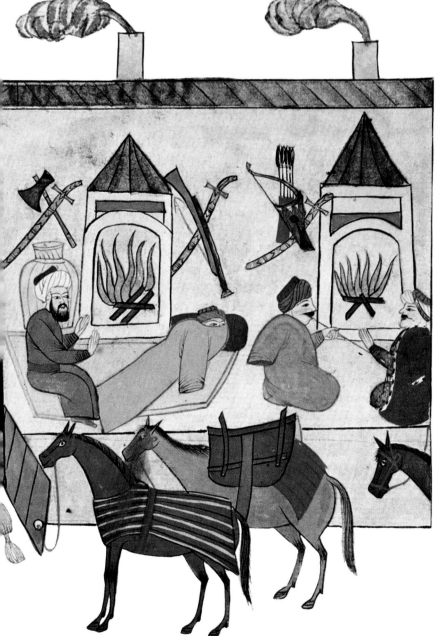

محفوظا اولوب درزدار مزبورک سعی و هتمام و دلیرانه اقدامنه

مزبورک سعی و هتمام و دلیرانه اقدامنه

حصار پیکولی

sultan was to order Prince Lazar brought before him and killed.

Bayezid I, who was proclaimed the new sultan while still at Kosovo, opened his reign with a barbarous act that presaged the inflexibility and ruthlessness which marked the dynasty. He ordered that his brother, Yakub, be immediately put to death by strangulation with a bowstring. The motive was simple: Death was the most certain way of ensuring that one's brother would never rebel and claim the throne. The Islamic belief that there exists only one sovereign on earth as there is but one God in heaven would thus remain unviolated.

Vain, impetuous, and arrogant, Bayezid was nevertheless a brilliant military leader. His subjects called him *Yilderim* (Lightning Bolt) in acknowledgment of his decisive victories, his swift moving armies, and his unpredictability. He reduced Serbia to vassalage once more, taking a daughter of Lazar as a wife, and his armies ranged from the Danube to the Peloponnesus. Conquering more territory in Anatolia, he failed to assimilate his new Moslem subjects properly, preferring the luxuries of his court to the rigors of statesmanship. Losing patience with the chronic insubordination of his numerous Byzantine vassals, he laid siege to isolated Constantinople. Some of the Byzantine officials who had crossed him had

their hands cut off; others were blinded.

In 1396, Bayezid broke off the siege to confront a new threat. Western knights and nobles, most of them from France, had joined forces with King Sigismund of Hungary in a major crusade. The Crusaders, oblivious to the Turks, caroused down the Danube to Nicopolis, in Bulgaria, slaughtering men, women, and children on the way. Sigismund, who recognized the Turkish menace, urged a careful battle plan, but the noble French knights were greedy for glory. Charging recklessly at the Turks, seven hundred knights disposed of the untrained expendable rabble who were deployed, as usual, in front of the Ottoman army; at the crest of a hill, however, they suddenly found themselves overwhelmed by forty thousand well-trained Ottoman regulars. Bayezid's victory was quick, decisive, and merciless.

In his Anatolian campaign, Bayezid had attacked some of the vassals of the Tatar ruler Tamerlane (Timur the Lame), the Moslem who by the late 1300s had conquered most of central Asia. Tamerlane, in return, had issued him a warning. "Thou art no more than an ant," he wrote to the sultan, "why provoke the elephants?" Bayezid replied arrogantly with taunts and insults, and Tamerlane, after seizing Baghdad and Syria, struck west into Anatolia, where Bayezid was attempting to resume his partially

Left, Sultan Bayezid I entering Nicopolis, on the Danube in Bulgaria, after defeating French and Hungarian crusaders in 1396. The sultan kept a few captured knights as hostages and made them watch with him while hundreds of others were beheaded. The failure of this last grand crusade opened the way for the Turks to conquer Serbia, and by 1456 both the fortified monastery of Masanjo (above) and the fortress of Smederevo (right) were in Ottoman hands.

completed conquests. In 1402, at the battle of Ankara, it was Bayezid's turn to underestimate an Eastern enemy. Outmaneuvered by Tamerlane's superb tactics, deserted by many of his Anatolian troops, Bayezid went down to defeat. He was captured and, according to some legends, forced to kneel as a footstool for the gouty Tamerlane while his Serbian wife served naked at Tamerlane's table. The Tatars then chased the remnants of Bayezid's army into Europe, and the humiliated sultan died a few months later.

During the next ten years, as Bayezid's four sons battled for the succession to the throne, any outside attack would probably have destroyed the Ottomans forever. But Tamerlane had returned to the East, and the Europeans, having expended themselves at Nicopolis, did nothing. When Bayezid's youngest son emerged as the survivor of the civil war and was proclaimed Sultan Mohammed I in 1413, he began to reassemble the fragments of the shattered empire. That task was completed by his son, Murad II.

In 1444, after the Hungarian patriot John Hunyadi led a deep incursion into Ottoman territory, Murad arranged for a ten-year truce with the Hungarians and retired to Magnesia, in Asia Minor, to study and pray, leaving the affairs of state to his twelve-year-old son, Mohammed, and the grand vizier Halil Pasha. But the Hungarians violated the treaty immediately—arguing that oaths sworn to enemies of Christ need not be kept—and Murad had to hasten back to the throne to meet a new invasion. After surprising and roundly defeating Hunyadi on the Black Sea coast, Murad II once more retired—and once more was called back. This time, he turned his attentions to his precocious and willful son, who had been concocting a rash scheme to attack Constantinople in his father's absence.

Upon Murad's death in 1451, the headstrong ambitious youth who would eventually be known as Mohammed the Conqueror returned to the throne as Mohammed II. Now there was no one to check his ambition. After ordering the strangulation of his infant half brother, Mohammed single-mindedly marshaled his forces to capture the prize that had for so long eluded his ghazi forebears. Constantinople's population, morale, and military forces had been drastically reduced, but it was still a formidable bastion. Mohammed first had to dominate both sides of the Bosporus, a remarkable achievement in itself. To accomplish that and to breach the city's walls he needed not only his large army but engineers, a new fleet, thousands of laborers, and up-to-date European cannons.

Late one night during the year and a half of preparation prior to the onset of the siege, Mohammed

Mohammed I (left) won a long civil war with the support of the janissaries, who called him "the most just and most virtuous of Ottoman princes." The Greek city of Salonika, which his grandfather had conquered, was lost to Byzantium during the civil war and then sold to Venice. Mohammed's son, Murad II, retook it in 1430, with great bloodshed. Christian churches in the city, such as the Hagia Dimitrios (right) and the Hagia Sophia with its Byzantine capitals (above), survived the wars and conquests. Top left, a bridge in Epirus, which fell to the Ottomans in 1499.

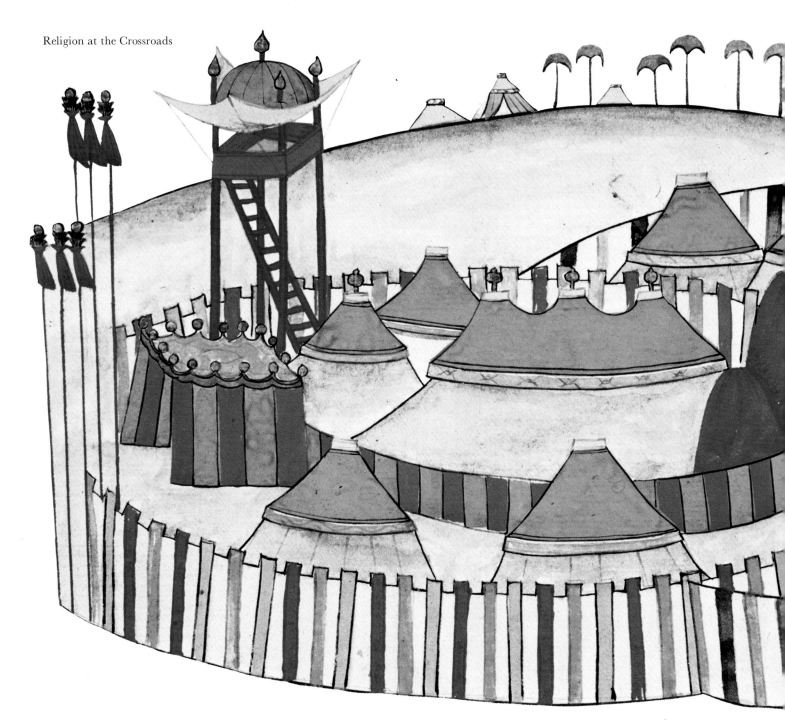

suddenly summoned the grand vizier Halil to his chambers. Halil, who had frustrated the impetuous adolescent during Mohammed's first two "reigns," thought his time had come and apprehensively brought along a dish of gold coins to appease the sultan. But Mohammed waved the offering away. "I want only one thing," he told Halil. "Give me Constantinople." A few weeks after the siege began, as the Byzantines stoutly withstood the Turkish attack, Halil advised Mohammed to break it off; after the city fell Halil was accused of treachery and was promptly executed.

Refusing all of Mohammed's holy war surrender demands (based on complete surrender to Allah in exchange for the sparing of lives), Constantinople withstood the siege for seven weeks. Finally, early on May 29, 1453, the great walls were breached, and the Ottomans broke through the gaps. As his troops pil-

laged the city, Mohammed rode to the church of Hagia Sophia, perhaps the greatest in Christendom, from which many of the city's residents had already been borne off as prisoners and slaves. He declared the church a mosque, an imam (or prayer leader) recited the Moslem creed from the pulpit, and Mohammed mounted the altar and bowed to Allah.

To the Europeans, the fall of Constantinople confirmed that the Ottoman Empire was a European power, henceforth to be valued as an ally. In the eyes of the Moslem East, victory conferred a new prestige on the Ottomans, for they had succeeded where the old Arab caliphs had failed. And to the Ottomans themselves, the triumph united their Asian and European domains and completed their transformation from ghazi band to empire. Mohammed had always considered himself a combination of the Roman Caesars and Alexander the Great; now, at the age of

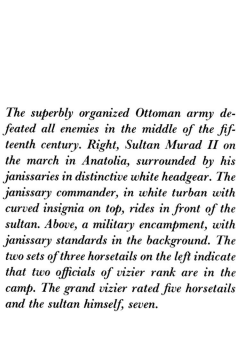

*The superbly organized Ottoman army de-
feated all enemies in the middle of the fifteenth century. Right, Sultan Murad II on
the march in Anatolia, surrounded by his
janissaries in distinctive white headgear. The
janissary commander, in white turban with
curved insignia on top, rides in front of the
sultan. Above, a military encampment, with
janissary standards in the background. The
two sets of three horsetails on the left indicate
that two officials of vizier rank are in the
camp. The grand vizier rated five horsetails
and the sultan himself, seven.*

The fall of Constantinople

Previous Ottoman sieges of Constantinople failed because the city could be resupplied by sea. Well aware of this, Mohammed II built a new fort on the European side of the Bosporus before beginning his assault, thus enabling him to control the waterway and block the seaward approaches. His attempts to sail his fleet of 125 vessels into the harbor of the Golden Horn, however, were frustrated by a chain of wooden floats across the harbor mouth. So, to the city's consternation, the fleet was hauled overland on wheeled cradles moving on greased timbers and drawn by hundreds of oxen. On the landward side, an Ottoman cannon tore gaps in the thick walls; the seven thousand defending troops built stockades across the gaps and beat back Turkish attempts to scale them for weeks. At length, the cannon breached the stockade, and the janissaries, or "new troops," poured through. After hours of desperate fighting, in which the last Byzantine emperor died incognito, Constantinople was overcome.

Mohammed II (left), known as Mohammed the Conqueror, spared no expense to equip his forces with the most modern weapons available. Yet he appreciated the arts of peace as much as he did the arts of war. After leading his troops into Constantinople (right), Mohammed found one of his soldiers trying to remove part of the marble floor of the church of Hagia Sophia. The sultan struck the man with his sword, saying, "For you the treasures and the prisoners are enough; the buildings fall to me." He preserved many of the city's art works and commissioned new ones. Below, a sixteenth-century view of Constantinople and its harbor, the Golden Horn, as seen from the Asian shore of the Bosporus.

To crack the massive walls (center right), Mohammed hired an armorer to cast huge bronze cannons (right). The biggest gun was twenty-six feet long, fired half-ton cannonballs, and required seven hundred men and thirty oxen for transport. From the Castle of Rumeli Hisari (top right), built to control the Bosporus, smaller cannons sank Venetian ships trying to bring grain to the city.

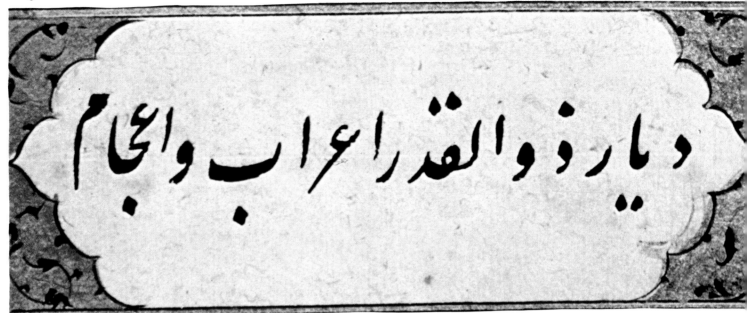

دیاردوالقدراعراب واعجام

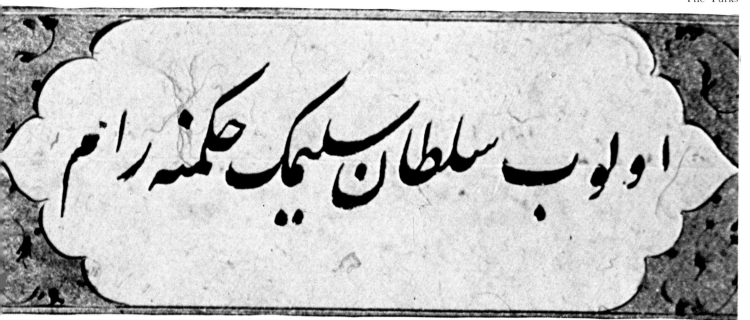

اولوب سلطان سليمك حكمنه رام

Above, a scroll bearing the name of Selim I. Immediately after his ascension ceremony (left), Selim ordered his brothers and nephews strangled. Despite his brutality, he wrote poetry in Persian and took bards along on his campaigns to record his exploits. When he conquered the old Moslem world, the standard and cloak of the prophet Mohammed were transferred to Istanbul, symbolizing Ottoman authority over all Islam.

twenty-one, he was well on his way to proving it.

Mohammed moved his capital to Constantinople, renamed it Istanbul (a Turkish rendition of the Greek words "to the city"), and set about restoring its imperial glory under his Islamic rule. He built new palaces, schools, bazaars, hospitals, and inns, and ordered a majestic new mosque for himself. He urged former residents of the city to return, promising them safety and tax concessions, and he imported artisans, craftsmen, and men of learning from all parts of his empire, even inviting the Venetian painter Bellini to spend a year in Istanbul.

After Constantinople, Athens fell to Mohammed's forces, as did the Greek peninsula and the entire southern shore of the Black Sea. His army and growing navy captured the Danube delta and invaded the Crimea, where a Genoese slave market and the territory of a Tatar khan came under his domain. He pushed back a Turkoman ruler from Iran, Uzun Hassan, who attacked deep into Anatolia along Tamerlane's old route. In the aftermath of that campaign the Ottomans gained control of the Asia Minor peninsula. Success, however, was not always forthcoming to Mohammed. When he led a large expedition to take Belgrade, Murad II's old foe Hunyadi tricked Mohammed into thinking the city was deserted. As the janissaries ran through it at night look-ing for plunder, thousands of Hungarians stormed out of hiding places on signal and slaughtered the elite Ottoman soldiers before they could form ranks. The island of Rhodes, a colony of the Knights Hospitallers of Saint John (a Christian religious and military order) since the early crusades, likewise withstood an Ottoman assault.

Venice had long held a virtual monopoly on western Europe's trade with the East, trade which Mohammed wanted to control. Accordingly, in 1463, he opened a land route across the Balkan peninsula to Ragusa (now Dubrovnik), threatening the Venetian maritime monopoly. War with Venice broke out the same year. After an exhausting series of long and bloody campaigns and sieges, the Ottomans subdued Albania. Bosnia was conquered and converted to Islam, and from there the Turks advanced around the head of the Adriatic. In 1477 and 1478, they twice raided so close to Venice that the smoke from burning villages could be seen from the campanile of St. Mark's Cathedral. At this point, the Venetians appealed for peace, agreeing to pay tribute and to give up many of their islands and strongholds on the eastern shore of the Adriatic. In return, they regained the right to trade within the Ottoman Empire.

When Mohammed died in 1481, his son Bayezid II became sultan by bribing the janissaries to support him against his brother—a tactic that soon became customary. Bayezid II built up the Ottoman navy and, renewing the conflict with Venice, captured more of the remaining Venetian ports in southern Greece. Then another menace from Asia diverted his attention to the Moslem world and led to another great surge of Turkish conquest.

In 1502, a religious leader named Ismail Safavi had proclaimed himself shah of Iran. He preached the mystical Shi'ite brand of Islam, which was regarded

Ottoman power and wealth peaked during the reign of Suleiman I (left). The slave who dressed him put twenty gold ducats and a thousand silver pieces in the pockets of his master's silk caftan every morning and was rewarded with the robe and the remaining coins at night. In 1526, after his victory at Mohács (right) over King Louis of Hungary, Suleiman wrote in his diary, "The sultan on a golden throne receives homage. . . . Massacre of two thousand prisoners. . . ." Above, jeweled brooch on a sultan's turban.

as heresy by the Orthodox Sunnite Ottomans, and his heretical beliefs spread among the Turkoman nomads in eastern Anatolia, who had always resisted Ottoman attempts to control them. Incited and supported by Shah Ismail, the Turkomans invaded Anatolia, and the Persian Shi'ite doctrines began to take hold among the Ottoman subjects. Even the sultan's favorite son embraced Shi'ism and put on the *kizilbash,* the red hat of the heretics.

That was too much for Bayezid II's fanatic and warlike youngest son, Selim. Enlisting the support of the janissaries by promising them new conquests, Selim forced his father to abdicate in his favor in 1512, and proclaimed a ghazi holy war against the heretics. After slaying forty thousand wearers of the kizilbash in Anatolia, Selim led his armies against Shah Ismail. The Ottomans were now armed with muskets—the new European weapon—and Kurdistan, Azerbaijan, and Tabriz fell under their onslaught. Ismail's Persian army was crushed.

Selim then marched south against the heartland of

the old Moslem world, which was ruled from Cairo by the Mameluke dynasty. At Aleppo, in Syria, he defeated the Mameluke sultan and went on to take Damascus, Beirut, and Jerusalem. By the time he arrived in Egypt, he had also captured the last Abbassid caliph, the titular religious leader of Orthodox Islam who had been living under Mameluke protection. The caliph acknowledged Ottoman predominance, and Selim took Cairo after a few days' fighting against Mameluke troops. He thus gained control of Egypt and the Mameluke domains, including the holy cities of Mecca and Medina.

In his reign of eight years, Selim nearly doubled the size of the Ottoman Empire without once fighting the Europeans. In the same brief span, he fired and beheaded seven of his grand viziers. The inevitable beheadings gave rise to a sardonic Turkish curse, "Mayest thou be Selim's vizier," meaning "May you be struck dead." In the West, he is remembered as Selim the Grim. There is some doubt that Selim formally assumed the title of caliph, but by force of arms

Administration and justice

The Ottomans regarded the equitable administration of justice as the most important function of government, primarily for practical reasons. Justice was necessary for public order, and public order was essential to produce revenue, which was needed to maintain the military force without which holy war—the ultimate purpose of the state—could not be waged. The highest organ of the Ottoman government, the imperial council, or *divan,* was essentially a court overseeing justice at the highest level. It evolved from the old tradition of a ruler listening to complaints, adjudicating disputes, and punishing wrong-doers. In the early days of the empire, the sultan himself presided at these public sessions of the divan; later the grand vizier officiated and made judgments in the sultan's name. In the classic period of the empire, under Suleiman the Magnificent, the divan met as a court in the mornings and privately discussed other government business in the afternoon. Although punishments were harsh—amputation of a hand for horse-thievery, for example—swift and impartial justice was administered by the network of judges, or *kadis,* independent of local authority and responsible directly to the sultan. No one could be punished unless convicted by a kadi. The kadis were *ulema,* learned men of Islam, and they were responsible for upholding both the Islamic law of the Koran and the secular decrees of the sultan. Non-Moslems were not subject to Islamic law and were usually tried and punished by leaders of their own respective communities.

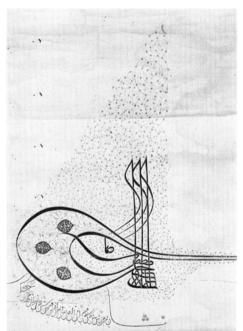

Left, the grand vizier presiding over a court session of the imperial council. The three small figures in the foreground, guarded by a military officer, are the accused. The sultan himself sometimes observed the proceedings through the latticed window in the back wall, as he is doing here. The cases handled directly by the imperial council generally concerned affairs of the central administration—such as the group execution of 150 treasury officers for malfeasance. Judicial verdicts of the council and all decrees of the sultan were stamped with the sultan's seal, or tughra *(above), a calligraphic representation of the thumb print of an early sultan who could not sign his name. Right, miniatures showing some of the particularly horrible methods of execution practiced by the Ottomans on domestic criminals and irksome foreign enemies. Needless to say, this public cruelty encouraged enemies to submit to Allah and, once under Ottoman rule, to obey the laws.*

The Danube (right) was both a barrier to and a highway for Ottoman expansion. Several sultans sent boats up the river to support their armies. Suleiman I seized Intep (above) along this route. In 1521, he captured Belgrade, where the fortress of Kalemegdan (below) is now a military museum. Belgrade remained under Turkish rule until 1718.

he became the most powerful monarch in the Moslem world and the acknowledged ruler of Islam. He also fathered the greatest Ottoman sultan of all.

Suleiman the Magnificent, as he came to be known, was twenty-six when he ascended the throne in 1520. He had received a rigorous education in the palace schools, had gained administrative experience by serving as governor in three provinces, and exhibited intelligence and insight as well as practicality. From the beginning of his reign, Suleiman realized that he had the strength and position to play power politics with the great divisive states of Europe. His alliance with France, for instance, set the pattern for the balance of diplomatic power in which Turkey and France were teamed against other European powers for many years.

Suleiman's first military move was to seize the prizes that had eluded Mohammed the Conqueror: Because of Hungarian disunity, Belgrade fell to Ottoman cannoneers and janissaries in 1521 after its defenders had set it afire; a year later, the Knights Hospitallers of Saint John were finally expelled from the island of Rhodes after a long and bloody siege.

The fertile and strategically valuable plains of Hungary beckoned as the next obvious objective. The Turks' old enemy, Hungary, was engaged in a civil war over the question of Hapsburg rule; Vienna lay just beyond as Europe's only remaining protection against Ottoman forces, and Suleiman's janissaries were so eager for adventure and plunder that they united in protest against peace. In addition, King Francis I of France, who had been captured in battle by the Hapsburg Holy Roman emperor, smuggled out a message to Istanbul suggesting an alliance and asking the sultan to attack the Hapsburgs through Hungary.

Suleiman was only too happy to oblige, and the long Franco-Turkish alliance started out auspiciously. In 1526, Suleiman's army met that of King

Life in the Ottoman court

Attended night and day by courtiers meticulously trained for their specialized tasks, the sultan lived in splendor befitting his wealth and power. His courtiers, from grand vizier down to the page who poured his perfumed drinking water, were his slaves.

Much of his day was occupied with formal meetings with his viziers, for until the seventeenth century, the sultans ruled as well as reigned. Everyone at court dressed and cut their beards in a prescribed manner: Viziers wore green, for example, and chamberlains wore scarlet. In his leisure, the sultan could admire the rare birds and herds of wild animals in his private gardens, or call for wrestlers, jesters, dancers,

or poets to amuse him. Or he might practice his own craft, for the sultans also studied in the palace schools. Suleiman the Magnificent was an accomplished goldsmith, and Mohammed the Conqueror was

a gardener so proud of his cucumbers that he cut open the stomach of the slave-gardener suspected of stealing a particularly fine one (the imperial cucumber had indeed been eaten).

Far left, a sultan surrounded by his court. Besides the viziers, the important functionaries were the judges, the accountants, the state secretaries, and the janissary commander. Any of them could be executed at the sultan's whim. Normally the sultan reclined on low cushions; the golden throne set with topazes (left) was used for formal occasions. No one could eat when the sultan dined (right). There were special pages to serve each course and a doctor stood by—in case of poisoning.

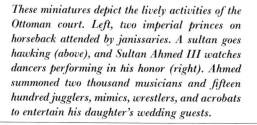

These miniatures depict the lively activities of the Ottoman court. Left, two imperial princes on horseback attended by janissaries. A sultan goes hawking (above), and Sultan Ahmed III watches dancers performing in his honor (right). Ahmed summoned two thousand musicians and fifteen hundred jugglers, mimics, wrestlers, and acrobats to entertain his daughter's wedding guests.

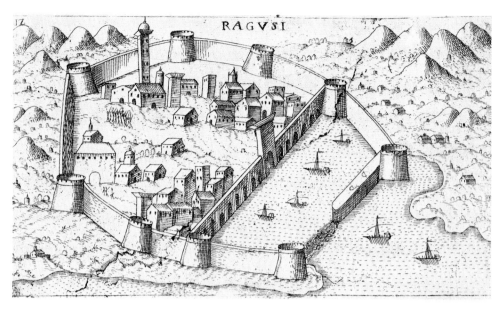

Louis of Hungary at Mohács, on the Danube halfway between Belgrade and the Hungarian capital of Buda. The Hungarians were defeated in an hour and Louis himself died on the battlefield with twenty-four thousand of his countrymen. When overcome by ill fortune, Hungarians still remark "No matter, more was lost on Mohács' field."

After plundering Buda and Pest, the Turks withdrew and left the Hungarians free to attend to civil war, during which a Hapsburg defeated the Ottoman client. Suleiman came back in 1529 to take on the

Above right, a sixteenth-century print of the Adriatic port of Ragusa, now Dubrovnik, an early Ottoman trading partner. After 1463, silks, spices, and wheat from Istanbul and Bursa were carried overland across the Balkans to Ragusa and then shipped through the papal states to Florence and western Europe in exchange for gold and Florentine woolens. This trade competed with the maritime commerce of Venice and flourished particularly during the Ottoman-Venetian wars. Although Ragusa was an Ottoman vassal, the little state joined some of the Christian alliances against the Turks, which may have accounted for the beheading (right) of a Ragusan ambassador at the sultan's court. Above, a firman, or edict, granting Ragusa commercial privileges. The sultan's tughra, or seal, is at the top.

Venice (right) and Genoa (below right) competed for eastern Mediterranean trade until Venice gained supremacy in 1380. Thereafter, Genoa tended to ally with the Turks, while Venice alternately struggled against them and negotiated treaties to obtain the right to trade in the empire and to purchase Balkan wheat.

Hapsburg Holy Roman Empire—which was again warring with France—and to besiege Vienna. Protestants and Catholics buried their differences to meet this bold Turkish advance. The troops defending Vienna, the grandest city of central Europe, were the well-armed veterans of Emperor Charles V's campaigns, and they made expert preparations for a long siege. But it was autumn, and the Turks could not mount a lengthy contest. Because they depended on forage to feed their horses, their cavalry was useless in winter. Furthermore, heavy rains had damaged their morale and deprived them of one of their strongest weapons—their mammoth cannon. For three weeks, Suleiman's soldiers hurled arrows, musket balls, and themselves at Vienna's walls before retreating, beaten as much by the weather as by the enemy. Vienna was Suleiman's only major military setback and it marked the limit of the Ottoman advance on the European continent. Suleiman won many battles against the Hapsburgs in the next three decades; he forced them to give up territory and to pay him tribute. But he never again attacked Vienna.

On the sea, the Ottoman successes continued. Barbarossa, the famed corsair of North Africa, had already terrorized the Mediterranean when Suleiman appointed him grand admiral of the Turkish navy in 1533. Enlarged and reorganized under Barbarossa's direction, the fleet extended the Ottoman domain throughout most of the north coast of Africa. The Ottoman navy also sniped at Italy, Spain, Gibraltar, and the Venetian islands of the Ionian Sea. Cooperating with the French fleet, the Turkish navy kept the Spanish and Italian ships of the Holy Roman Empire bottled up in the western Mediterranean. In the battle of Preveza, fought off the Albanian coast in September of 1538, the Genoese seaman-turned-naval-leader Andrea Doria commanded an unsuccessful allied European attack against the Ottomans. The Turks now ruled the eastern Mediterranean.

After 1541, problems in the East turned Suleiman's attention away from Europe. As the French kings sought to relieve Hapsburg pressure on France by urging the Turks to attack central Europe, so did the Hapsburgs form an alliance with Persia to relieve the Ottoman pressure on them. Suleiman was forced to

lead three campaigns against the Persian shahs, during which he overran Georgia and Armenia, took Baghdad, and reached the Persian Gulf. He also built a new fleet to sail the Indian Ocean, and challenged the Portuguese, whose sea route around Africa had cut the Ottomans out of east-west trade. Although partially able to restore old trade routes through the Middle East, the Ottomans were unable to break the Portuguese control of the Indian Ocean, and therefore lost their previous stature in international trade.

At the same time the Turks were fighting for control abroad, the Ottoman Empire was also undergoing major internal changes. In the 1536 treaty formalizing the alliance with France, French merchants and diplomats residing in Ottoman territory were granted the right to be governed by their own laws and tried by their own courts. Such privileges, soon obtained by other Europeans, were to trouble the Ottomans later, but at the time they seemed harmless to the powerful

Ottoman state, which was subsidizing France. These "capitulations," as they were called, agreed perfectly with the Ottoman principle that it is people who are governed, not territory. Not even Mohammed II cared to govern all the people in the territory he controlled. After the fall of Constantinople, he had established a system under which each religious minority was governed in religious and in some secular matters by its own religious leaders and laws. At the time, he chose a new Greek Orthodox patriarch and invested him with many of the ceremonial duties of the Byzantine emperors. An Armenian patriarch and a Jewish chief rabbi also managed the affairs of their flocks from Istanbul. As non-Moslems paid higher taxes than Moslems, the pragmatic Ottoman administration had no desire to convert large numbers of infidels.

Under Suleiman, the Ottoman administrative system reached its zenith of efficiency and zeal, bringing to the empire an era of power, wealth, justice, and cultural attainment. At the apex of the system was the sultan himself, an autocrat ruling by decree and holding the power of life or death over his subjects. The only legal check upon him was the Koran, as interpreted by the *ulema,* holy men of learning, who could—and later on did—depose a sultan.

Although the sultans maintained the ghazi and nomad tradition of leading their troops in battle and bringing along their top advisers on expeditions, the sultan's court in Istanbul took on much of the ceremonial protocol of the Byzantines. From the time of Mohammed II, for example, it was the grand vizier—not the sultan—who presided over meetings of the *divan,* the imperial council. The grand vizier sat be-

fore a latticed window, known as the "eye of the sultan," through which the monarch could observe the proceedings when he chose. The deliberations of the divan were attended by the vizier for finance, the highest judges, the keeper of the seal, the *aga* (commander) of the janissaries, the grand admiral, and the chief secretary (later foreign minister). Each represented a huge bureaucracy and all were responsible for the proper observance of a multitude of laws and detailed regulations.

These officials and their subordinates were slaves of the sultan, drafted and indoctrinated like the janissaries. Selected for intelligence and aptitude, given

The harem

The harem—a word of Arabic origin meaning sacred or prohibited—has long fascinated the West. But the fanciful picture of a helpless, obedient damsel did not always fit the Turkish concubine. The mother of the reigning sultan, the *sultana valide,* dominated the harem, and for a long period in the sixteenth and seventeenth centuries, a series of determined sultana valides dominated the sultans and their governments as well. The harem women were carefully selected for beauty and brains from the slave markets and the prisoners of war. They were educated and trained in the palace schools and had to rise through a hierarchy of ranks before they could even look at the sultan. Those who bore the sultan's children were given special privileges and private living accommodations, and the first to bear a son to a sultan took precedence over the others.

The harem section (above) of the Topkapi palace overlooked the Bosporus (above, far right). Except for the sultan, his sons, and the black eunuchs who guarded the harem and enforced its regulations, no man could pass through the harem's ornate, mother-of-pearl doors (below, far right), and no harem woman could leave without special permission, which was rarely given. Below, the sultan visiting the harem accompanied by his mother and the chief black eunuch. The sultan's mother selected the group from which the sultan chose his odalisques, or concubines. A favorite, such as this dancer (right), could become wealthy and challenge the sultana valide for influence. Below right, a now-silent cloister of the harem. The palace has become a museum.

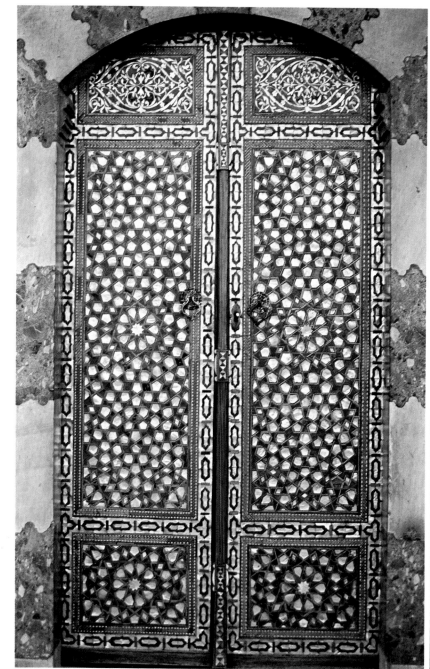

For three centuries, the Turks and the Venetians battled for the islands around Greece. Of particular importance were Lemnos and Tennedos, which commanded the entrance to the Dardanelles and changed rulers many times. As Ottoman power declined in the seventeenth century, the Venetians captured Lemnos (top, far right), but a few years later, in 1657, the Turks, under Grand Vizier Mohammed Koprulu, regained control (above). In 1537, the fortress of Corfu (bottom, far right) successfully withstood a siege by the Ottoman navy after a battle (right) with a Christian fleet.

the best and most rigorous education in the palace schools, insulated from outside ties and loyalties, promoted on the basis of merit alone, the slave-bureaucrats assured the efficiency, the loyalty, and the incorruptibility of the machinery of state. After Halil Pasha, the last grand vizier from the old noble Turkish families, even the grand viziers whose loyalties were above suspicion were almost all products of the slave system.

The palace schools also played a key role in the cultural life of the empire, shaping the styles of the skilled artists and craftsmen who gravitated to Istanbul from all over the empire and from Europe and Persia. Sinan, the architect whose graceful domed mosques changed the skyline of the city, was a slave. So were some of the poets who composed epics in the flowery Persian style, and the doctors, the scholars, and the artisans. There were also primary schools and free colleges, or *medreses,* for the Moslem boys, many of which were founded by Suleiman. The medreses, supervised by the mosques, taught such secular subjects as logic, grammar, geometry, and astronomy, as well as Islamic philosophy. Higher academies prepared the most gifted students for careers as imams and teachers. No Renaissance city of western Europe could match Istanbul as a cosmopolitan center of culture and learning.

Even during the magnificent reign of Suleiman there were signs of corruption and eventual decay. Previous sultans had married foreign princesses who usually knew too little of Turkish customs and language to involve themselves in court intrigue. But in a break with precedent, Suleiman took as one of his four legal wives his favorite concubine from the harem, a Russian slave-girl named Roxelana. Edu-

The Barbary corsairs

The Ottomans became a major naval power by taking into their fold the North African Barbary pirates, of whom the most skillful and daring was Barbarossa. In 1533, Suleiman the Magnificent appointed Barbarossa grand admiral of the Ottoman navy and gave him a free hand to rebuild and enlarge the fleet. The next year, this new navy sailed through the Dardanelles, ravaged the coasts of Sicily and Italy, and captured Tunis. The Holy Roman emperor sent the Genoese admiral Andrea

were no match for the swift, oared galleys of Barbarossa. The Mediterranean had become a Turkish stronghold, and the Ottoman fleet raided as far as Gibraltar, visited France, and fought on the Riviera. Returning to Istanbul after one expedition, Barbarossa paraded his gifts for the sultan: two hundred slave boys dressed in scarlet, holding flasks of gold and silver; thirty more carrying purses of gold on their shoulders; two hundred men, each carrying a purse of money; and "two hundred infidels wearing collars, each bearing a roll of cloth on his back." In 1556, the father of the Turkish navy died of a fever in his palace in Istanbul.

Doria to retake Tunis with four hundred Spanish and Italian vessels, but Barbarossa escaped with his biggest galleys to raid the Balearic islands and bear off thousands of slaves and great quantities of Spanish treasure. Two years later, in 1536, the corsair plundered the Venetian islands of the Adriatic and around Greece. Once more Doria engaged him; the Christian fleet now included heavy square-rigged galleons, propelled entirely by sail, but they

Above, left and right, the rival admirals: Barbarossa, pirate and Ottoman pasha; and Andrea Doria, Genoese ruler and Hapsburg ally. Barbarossa brought the entire coast of North Africa under Ottoman dominion. In 1543, his Turkish galleys wintered in Marseille, where his French allies were shocked to see Christian slaves chained to oars. From there, the fleet captured and sacked Nice (right), which had been under the rule of the Italian House of Savoy.

Top, Turkish galleys grappling with a larger Venetian ship, a typical naval occurrence of the sixteenth century. Some of the corsair galleys (right) used sails as well as oars. Immediately above, a lookout tower in Corsica built to give warning of pirate raids.

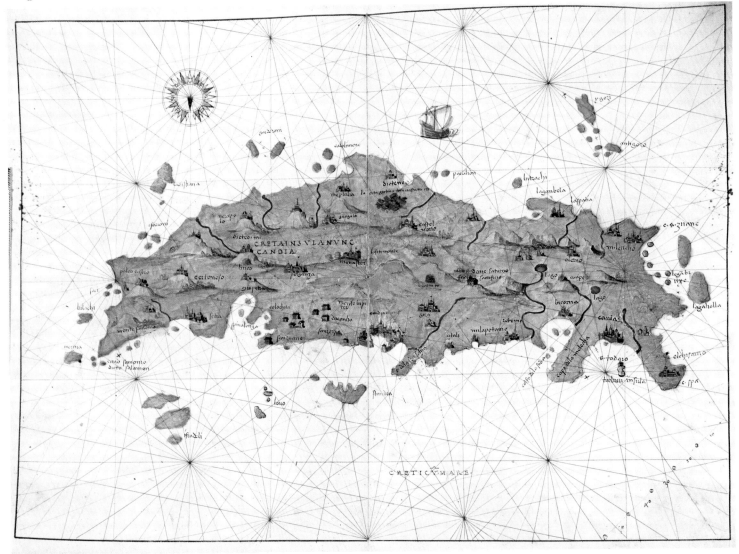

Cyprus, where crusader castles (left) still stand, and Crete were Venetian bastions until taken by the Turks. The Cyprus fortress of Famagusta (above) fell to an Ottoman invasion in 1571, and its Venetian commander was flayed alive. Crete (top) resisted the Turks for twenty-four years before succumbing in 1669. This sixteenth-century Venetian map of Crete shows north at the bottom; the standard convention of north at the top had not been established when the map was drawn.

cated in the harem branch of the palace schools, she became the first in a long series of *odalisques* (harem women who shared the sultan's bed) and *sultana valides* (mothers of reigning sultans), who intervened in court politics and government.

Roxelana's first act was to engineer the downfall of a grand vizier whose close relationship with the sultan she envied. She then maneuvered her son-in-law into the grand vizierate and with him plotted to make her son the next sultan. She accomplished this by convincing Suleiman that his chosen heir, his first-born son by his previous favorite, was plotting with the janissaries to overthrow him. Suleiman believed the tale and ordered the heir presumptive, his own son, strangled.

Suleiman was succeeded in 1566 by Roxelana's son, Selim II, a short, fat voluptuary who had no training for the job, who led no armies, and who did little more than live up to his nickname Selim the Sot. In his first edict, Selim II lifted the Islamic restrictions on the sale of wine. Thereafter, he left most of the affairs of empire to his father's last grand vizier, Sokollu Pasha. It thus fell to Sokollu to handle the Ottomans' tentative first encounter with Russia, the inevitable Ottoman enemy. Under Ivan the Terrible,

the Russians were expanding southward and encroaching on the Ottomans' Tatar vassals in the Crimea. In response, Sokollu sent an expedition to dig a canal between the Don and Volga rivers. It was an excellent idea, for it would have forestalled the Muscovites and enabled Turkish ships from the Black Sea to enter the Caspian Sea, thereby reopening the ancient Turkish caravan route through central Asia. But the canal was beyond the abilities of Sokollu's engineers, and the Turks, discouraged by the cold Russian steppes, withdrew. Nevertheless, the Russians were obliged to sign a treaty recognizing Ottoman rights to the Crimea.

Contrary to the advice of Sokollu, Sultan Selim ordered an invasion of Cyprus, still held by the Venetians. He had heard that Cyprus was known for its wine, and he was determined to obtain his share. In

In 1571, a Christian armada virtually destroyed the Ottoman navy at the famous battle of Lepanto (below), depicted here in a Venetian painting. Ecstatic Christians assumed that the battle marked the end of Turkish domination, but the Ottomans soon appeared on the seas with a new and bigger fleet.

Bazaars

Situated on the crossroads of the world, the Ottoman Empire drew much of its wealth from the taxes and customs duties it levied on trade between Europe and Asia. That trade focused on the bazaars. Every Ottoman city had its *bedestan,* or covered bazaar, which served not only as a center of retail trade but as headquarters of the great merchants whose trading ships and camel caravans brought goods directly to the bazaars. Each new arrival, whether of sellers or buyers, caused prices to fluctuate—which is why bazaar merchants haggled over price. Bedestans were often constructed around a complex of hospitals, schools, and a mosque, and the revenues from the bazaars supported the charitable institutions.

Although new wares may have been introduced from time to time, the lively, colorful atmosphere of the bazaars has changed little over the centuries. Left, a seventeenth-century Turkish miniature depicting a bazaar scene at the foot of the column of Arcadius in Istanbul. Above, three present-day views of Istanbul's central bazaar, where manufactured goods such as flashlight batteries and ballpoint pens are displayed as carefully as jewelry. In the time of Mohammed I, the central bedestan and the area around it contained more than a thousand shops.

To control and tax trade effectively, the sultans required that all the dealers in a particular commodity cluster together in the same part of the bazaar where expert inspectors could guard against smuggling and assure that honest measure was given. Above, a miniature showing the section of the bazaar reserved for the horse market. Permanent stalls (below right) were set up in covered avenues radiating from the center of the bedestans. Ottoman coins never bore the face of the sovereign, although each sultan struck new currency. Below left, gold coins of Suleiman II (left), Selim II (top), and Selim III (bottom).

response to the invasion of Cyprus, a huge armada of ships from Spain, Venice, Malta, the Papal States, and other Italian principalities sailed from Sicily to assault the Ottoman navy. The Christian fleet of two hundred galleys and thirty thousand fighting men was somewhat smaller than the Turkish force, but it was led by six mammoth Venetian *galleases,* vessels propelled by sails as well as oars, which were the largest ships yet seen in the Mediterranean. On October 7, 1571, at the Gulf of Lepanto on the west coast of Greece, the two fleets clashed in the last major battle fought by oared ships. In the center of the battleline, the flagships of the two commanders became locked together and for two hours boarding parties fought desperately on enemy decks. At length, the Turkish admiral was killed, his flagship captured, and several thousand Christian galley slaves in the Turkish ships broke free to seize weapons and turn on their captors. The Christians had won. More than two hundred Turkish galleys were sunk or captured.

Europe rejoiced at this first major Ottoman defeat, and for centuries the battle of Lepanto was glorified in song and story as the turning point in the centuries-old Christian struggle against Islam. In actuality, this was not the case. The "crusaders" fell to bickering again and failed to press their advantage by sailing into the defenseless Dardanelles. Within six

Elaborate pageants of floats, fireworks, and many kinds of displays always commemorated important events. In these miniatures, Sultan Murad III (above) watches the festivities (right) that celebrated the circumcision of his son. The large dummy figures represent European merchants in this circuslike atmosphere.

months Sokollu had built a new Turkish fleet, larger and stronger than the old. When it showed the flag on the Ionian Sea, the Venetians decided to cede Cyprus to the Turks and resume the business of trade.

Although the battle of Lepanto had not basically affected the empire, decline set in nevertheless. In 1574, Selim II came to an inglorious but fitting end: Drunk on Cyprus wine, he slipped in a bath and cracked his skull. His son and heir, Murad III, as obsessed with women and gold as his father had been with wine, had even less sense than his father—he prevented Sokollu from running the government. He undercut the grand vizier's power, then had him assassinated, thereby eliminating the only figure with the strength and authority to defend the empire from weak sultans, harem intrigues, rebellious janissaries, bureaucratic corruption, and economic turmoil.

The first ten sultans, from Osman through Suleiman, had reigned for nearly 280 years. In the next 140 years, starting with Selim the Sot, no less than thir-

a more humane policy was instituted when Ahmed I came to the throne in 1603.

The gentle policies of Ahmed, who is justly celebrated for the construction of Istanbul's famed Blue Mosque, turned out to be unfortunate for the empire. To eliminate the need for fratricide, it was decided during his reign to confine imperial princes all their lives to special quarters of the palace called the *kafes,* or cage. There they were brought up in indolence and luxury by the women of the harem and prevented from gaining any experience or forming any allegiances that would later enable them to rebel—or for that matter to govern. As they grew to manhood in the cage, they were permitted to take concubines, but these women were sterilized or their children were killed at birth to prevent the sultans from fathering sons before they ascended the throne. As a result, when sultans died their sons were often still children; and if they died with no male heir, they were suc-

teen sultans occupied the Ottoman throne. They lacked so completely the strong, warlike, dedicated spirit of the first ten that historians have wondered whether Selim really was Suleiman's son. Many of them were cowards, at least one was an imbecile, others were corrupt or debauched or psychotic. Only the fortuitous emergence of a few strong and able grand viziers managed to salvage the empire. Increasingly, the divan met in the grand vizier's official residence. This real seat of government was called Pasha's Gate and came to be known in the West as the Sublime Porte.

The era of weak sultans and strong concubines resulted from more than bad chance and bad bloodlines. Murad III spent so much time with various women that when his son Mohammed III came to the throne in 1595, he had nineteen brothers to kill— and he did not flinch at the task. Half a dozen pregnant odalisques who had been favorites of his brothers were also eliminated, as was one of Mohammed's own sons. Almost completely destroying the dynasty, this bloodbath so shocked Istanbul that

Left, facing Mecca under the 260 windows of the Blue Mosque (also shown on page 89), constructed in 1607 by Ahmed I (above). The first sultan to come to the throne without military or administrative experience, Ahmed I devoted himself to architectural and religious accomplishments and generally let his viziers rule. Right, a painted panel in which Arabic letters are used for decorative effect.

Fires of Istanbul

Fires were always a threat to the people of Istanbul. The great mosques and palaces and homes of the wealthy were built of stone, but the common people lived in wooden houses packed closely together, and they cooked on open hearths. Once a fire got started it was difficult to control, despite the activities of the well-organized fire brigades. A fire tower, manned night and day, was erected in the central part of the city, and the watchmen beat an enormous drum at the first sign of a blaze. Nevertheless, hardly a year went by in which some quarter of the city was not burned to the ground, often with hundreds of deaths occurring. Most of the fires were the result of accident or carelessness, but many were caused by arson, inspired by revenge, and some grew out of military revolts and disturbances arising from popular discontent.

Left and right, two miniatures of the period illustrating a great Istanbul fire of 1660. Even the minarets of a mosque (left) seem to have ignited on this occasion, but it was the wooden homes of the populace (right, foreground) that suffered most. Below, a miniature showing a stylized version of the bridge over the narrow end of the Golden Horn. Below right, the old Roman aqueduct of Istanbul as sketched by a Venetian traveler.

ceeded by a brother who was often terrified at emerging from his comfortable—but warped and debilitated—life in the kafes. In either case the sultana valide or the favorite concubine had no trouble taking over from the juvenile or incompetent sultan.

Ahmed also dealt a blow to the ghazi tradition of the state. The empire had been founded, organized, and inspired for holy war; that was its reason for existence. Until Ahmed's time, all truces and agreements with the Christian powers had been negotiated at the Ottoman court by envoys whom the Turks regarded as supplicants. The treaties always disparaged the foreign rulers (the Hapsburg emperor, for instance, was called "King of Vienna") and demanded that tribute be paid to the sultan. In this way, the ghazi tradition of infidels bowing to the power of Allah had been preserved, at least on parchment. But in making peace with Austria in 1606, after a long and inconclusive war, the Ottomans went to neutral territory to negotiate and sign a treaty in which, for the first time, the sultan formally agreed to treat a Christian sovereign "on a footing of equality." The Hapsburg emperor was given his title of "Kaiser" (Caesar) and tribute was ended. In conforming to the courtesies of diplomacy, Ahmed abandoned the ghazi beliefs; the soul of the empire would never be the same.

In the absence of the strong sultans they were meant to obey, the janissaries took power into their own hands, conspiring regularly with the harem to enthrone a particular prince and extorting huge sums for his support. They abandoned celibacy and started to father sons who inherited janissary status without the old janissary virtues. The presence of these freeborn Moslems in the ranks opened the way for other Moslems to enroll, swelling the corps to about two hundred thousand. Soon janissary certificates were being peddled and traded in the open market and presented for salary payments by holders who had no military function. In 1622, after an unsuccessful invasion of Poland had brought the wrath of the janissaries upon him, the adolescent Sultan Osman II tried valiantly to bring them into line by secretly

The second Turkish siege of Vienna, in 1683, was broken by a relief force under King John Sobieski of Poland (above left). In perfect formation, Sobieski's troops charged down a hillside upon the unfortified Ottoman encampment at the city's gates, and the Turks, commanded by Grand Vizier "Black Mustafa," were routed. Mustafa abandoned his tent (right) when he fled. Prince Eugene of Savoy (left) fought at Vienna and later, as a Hapsburg general, defeated the Turks again.

The rout of the Turks in 1683 was memorialized by paintings depicting the fighting around Vienna (left) and the victorious King John Sobieski in the middle of the fray (pages 140–141). At the sight of Sobieski charging at Grand Vizier Mustafa's tent, the Khan of the Tartars exclaimed, "By Allah, the King is really among us," and galloped off with his men. Panic spread, and the Ottoman army retreated, leaving ten thousand dead and great quantities of arms, jewelry, furs, and carpets on the battlefield. Mustafa escaped with his bullion and the Standard of the Prophet, but he was beheaded for his defeat nonetheless.

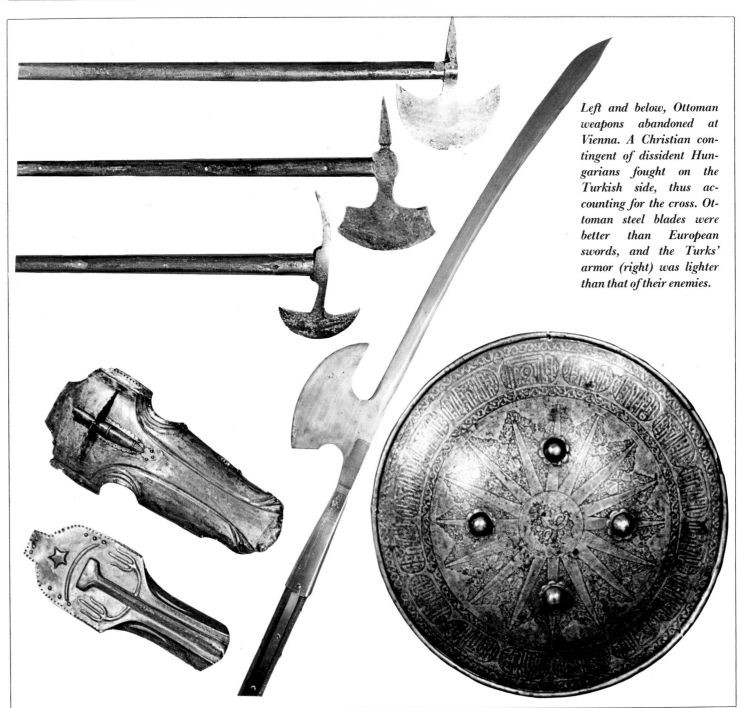

Left and below, Ottoman weapons abandoned at Vienna. A Christian contingent of dissident Hungarians fought on the Turkish side, thus accounting for the cross. Ottoman steel blades were better than European swords, and the Turks' armor (right) was lighter than that of their enemies.

raising a new militia in Asia. The janissaries discovered his plot and dethroned and killed him—the first but not the last regicide that was to occur in Ottoman history.

In addition to draining the treasury and creating chaos, janissary corruption and rebellion infected the whole government. If the elite janissaries, who had once epitomized loyalty and sacrifice, could scourge the state for their own gain, so could the bureaucrats, judges, or ulema. The merit system dissolved, promotions and appointments were purchased with favors or bribes, and the purchasers then recouped their investments by soliciting new bribes for themselves. Economic problems arising from outside causes aggravated the already existing internal decay. Government revenues declined because more and more east-west trade bypassed the empire by going around Africa and because fewer conquests meant less plunder. The cavalry, customarily awarded fiefs in conquered territory, became less important to the military, and so the system of fief-holding broke

down, further reducing the revenues of the central government; as most of the merchants were non-Moslems, no new bourgeois class like that of western Europe arose to reinforce the economic structure.

While the janissaries and the sepahis rampaged in the capital, the frontiers they should have been defending were crumbling. The Persians recaptured Baghdad, rebellions broke out in Asia Minor, North Africa, and the Crimea, and Russian Cossacks raided all around the Black Sea and approached Istanbul itself. At that point, in 1632, Sultan Murad IV broke free of his mother's domination, quelled a new military uprising that had killed his grand vizier, and checked the slide with a brutal reign of terror. On his orders, twenty-five thousand people were killed, many by his own hand. At first, only the rebels and the corrupt were executed, but soon after anyone even suspected of plotting or wrongdoing was killed. Finally, anyone who displeased the sultan in any way was forced to suffer a similar fate. His spies were everywhere and officials trembled and became speech-

The shifting boundaries of the Ottoman Empire

From its modest beginnings under Osman I, who declared his independence from the collapsing Seljuk Empire in 1290, the Ottoman state expanded rapidly to encompass most of Asia Minor and most of the Balkan Peninsula. In 1453, Mohammed II captured Constantinople, extending Ottoman dominion around the southwestern Black Sea.

At its height in the first half of the sixteenth century, the Ottoman Empire almost surrounded the Mediterranean. Under Selim I (1512–1520), the empire spread into Persia (1514), Syria and Egypt (1516 and 1517), and Algiers (1518). Suleiman the Magnificent (1520–1566) continued these gains, conquering Belgrade in 1521 and defeating the Hungarians at Mohács in 1526. In the East, he conquered Iraq and Armenia. Under subsequent sultans, setbacks alternated with small gains. One very costly loss occurred in 1683, when Mohammed IV's grand vizier, Kara Mustafa, failed to take Vienna. This marked the end of Turkish expansion into Europe.

More losses followed under the reigns of Suleiman II, Ahmed II, and Mustafa II. During the reign of Ahmed III (1703–1730), Greece and Crete were added to the empire, but parts of Wallachia, Hungary, and northern Serbia were lost. These latter areas were ceded to Austria under the Treaty of Passarowitz, which was signed in 1718.

Mehmed III

Although the Ottomans regained the territory lost in 1718 with the Peace of Belgrade of 1739, they were unable to halt their decline. A long series of conflicts with the Russians, the Russo-Turkish Wars, further weakened the empire, costing it the northern and northeastern coasts of the Black Sea. Under Selim III (1789–1807), rebellions in Serbia and Arabia, clashes with Napoleon, another war with Russia, and a revolt of the janissaries, continued to

The Ottoman Empire at about 1335
The Ottoman Empire at about 1453

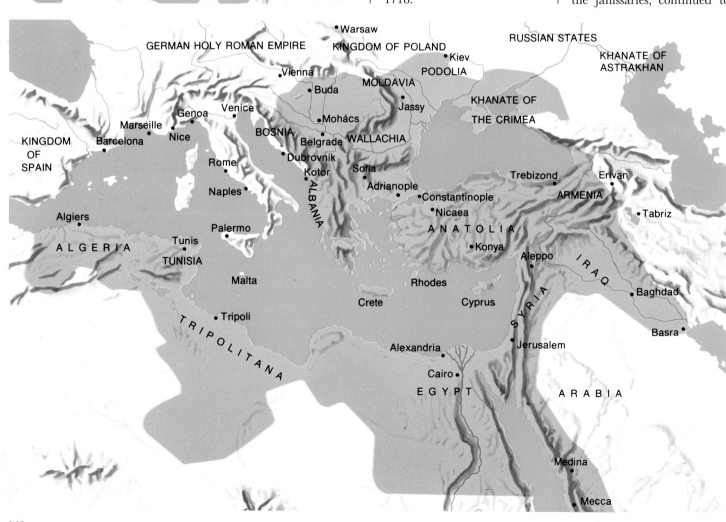

Osman II

Murad IV

Osman III

Selim III

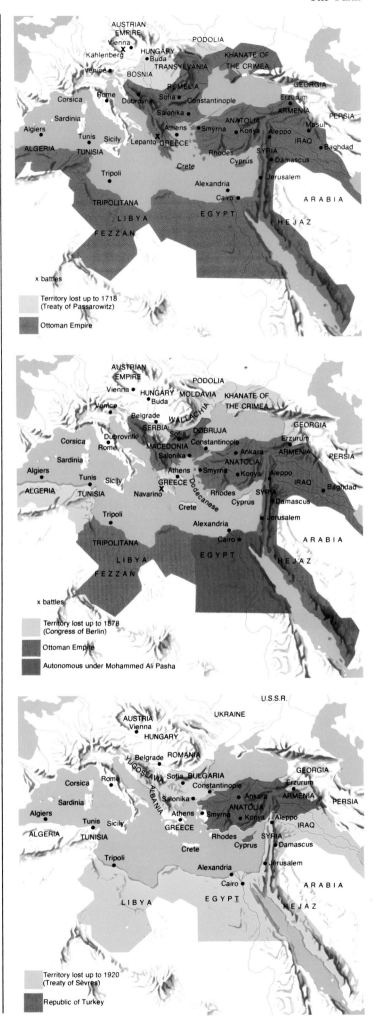

x battles

Territory lost up to 1718
(Treaty of Passarowitz)

Ottoman Empire

x battles

Territory lost up to 1878
(Congress of Berlin)

Ottoman Empire

Autonomous under Mohammed Ali Pasha

Territory lost up to 1920
(Treaty of Sèvres)

Republic of Turkey

paralyze the empire. Egypt became almost autonomous under Mohammed Ali Pasha, and the French conquered Algeria. Sultan Mahmud II (1808–1839) struggled to restore Ottoman supremacy, regaining Serbia in 1813, attempting to suppress the Greeks in their war for independence (1821–1829), and at home defeating the long-threatening janissaries (1826). Then British, Russian, and French intervention led to the destruction of the Egyptian (at that time an Ottoman ally) fleet at Navarino (1827) and the independence of Greece (1832). Later Ibrahim Pasha invaded Syria with Egyptian forces and almost succeeded in taking Constantinople. At Mahmud's death in 1839, Egypt became virtually independent. The reigns of Abdul-Aziz (1861–1876) and Abdul-Hamid (1876–1909) saw revolts in Serbia, Bulgaria, and Bosnia, while from within the empire, the Young Turks movement, opposed to the old government,

arose and grew. The Russo-Turkish War of 1877–1878 was a disaster for the Ottoman Empire, and in spite of the mitigating Congress of Berlin (1878), Romania, Serbia, and Montenegro became independent, and Bosnia-Hercegovina passed under Austrian administration.

In 1908, Bulgaria declared its independence, and losses continued under Mohammed V (1909–1918) with the loss of Libya to Italy in 1912, and the loss of almost all the remaining European territories in the Balkan Wars of 1912–1913. Turkish participation and defeat in the First World War completed the demise of the empire. Turkish nationalists overthrew the last sultan, Mohammed VI, in 1922, and in 1923 Mustafa Kemal was elected president of the Republic of Turkey.

Left, miniatures from the Topkapi Museum in Istanbul, depicting Sultans Suleiman II, Ahmed II, and Mustafa II, who reigned consecutively from 1687 to 1703. Although on the defensive by 1715, the Turks fought a successful war against Venice. However, their siege of Corfu (below) was a failure.

less at his approach. But they behaved. Having restored military discipline and a measure of adminstrative honesty, Murad led his armies on two successful campaigns in Asia, where he recaptured Baghdad and spread death and obedience throughout his realm.

After the death of the "bloody sultan" in 1640, another military revolt deposed and killed his successor, and the mother and the grandmother of the new boy sultan, Mohammed IV, struggled for power. Anarchy reigned in Istanbul as a Venetian fleet block-

aded the Dardanelles, cutting off much of the capital's food supply. In 1656, the sultan's mother arranged the strangulation of her mother-in-law and appointed a man of true ability to the post of grand vizier. Insisting on absolute power, even over the sultan, Mohammed Koprulu Pasha ruthlessly and efficiently weeded out corruption, put the finances in order, drove the Venetians from the Dardanelles, and strengthened the frontier with Russia. When he died, his son Ahmed Koprulu took over the Porte and kept the revival going by capturing Crete, taking part of

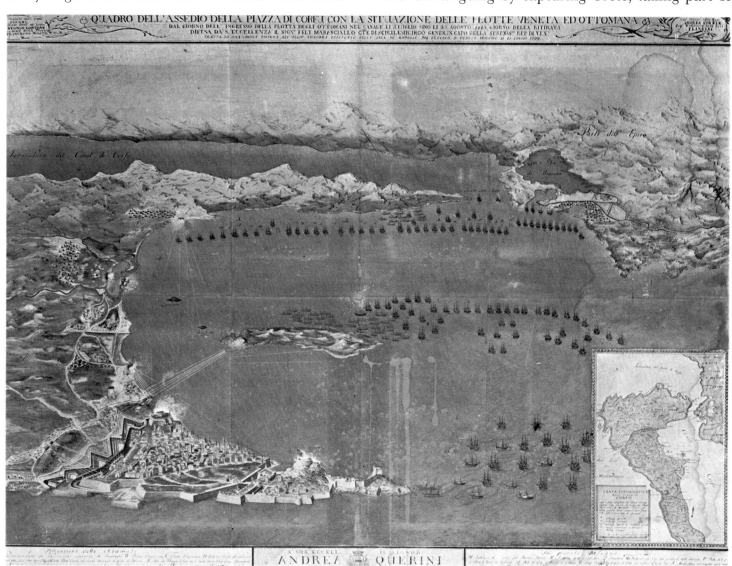

Ahmed III (left) reigned from 1703 to 1730. The boundaries of his empire were shrinking, but the sultan was an aesthete who encouraged literature and the arts and sciences of the West. He built a new library (above) for the Topkapi palace and embellished Istanbul with artificial lakes, pavilions, and kiosks, many in the French style. From his fountain (below), passersby could fill their jugs with water or get bronze cups of a sherbetlike ice in the summertime.

the Ukraine from Poland, and leading another Ottoman expedition through Hungary and Transylvania. Although his army was defeated by the Austrians, he managed to negotiate a favorable peace treaty with them by shrewd diplomacy.

In 1683, under the command of a belligerent, ambitious grand vizier called Kara Mustafa, or "Black Mustafa," whose abilities did not match his dreams, the Turks marched once more on Vienna, again encouraged by a king of France. This time it was purely poor leadership that defeated them. In the midst of the siege, with the defenders hard-pressed, a Christian reinforcing army under Poland's King John Sobieski

arrived on the heights above the city, on the hill of Kahlenberg. Mustafa, intent on the siege, had failed to deploy troops to protect his forces, which became trapped in a crossfire between the city and the relief force. When Sobieski led a charge into the center of the Turkish camp, Mustafa and the survivors of his army fled. The defeated Mustafa was put to death on the sultan's orders and with him died the long era of Turkish conquest.

The once fearsome Ottoman armies had been outstripped by the strong new nation-states of Europe. Budapest and Hungary were soon lost, the Venetians grabbed back parts of Greece, and Czar Peter the

Treasures of Topkapi

The Topkapi palace, home of the Ottoman sultans for nearly five centuries, is now a museum containing the finest artistic treasures that they commissioned, captured as war booty, or received as tribute. Islamic art is essentially an art of ornamentation. Simple primary forms were dominant in the early days, and naturalism was not prevalent until relatively recently. Forbidden by the Koran to represent the human form, Turkish artists achieved impressive decorative effects with floral motifs and the letters of the Arabic script. The treasures of Topkapi are varied in style as they reflect the many centuries of the empire and the various influences that affected its culture. These precious objects testify to the immense wealth of the sultans and to their desire to have gold and jewels adorning their bodies, their clothing, and their dwellings. Such costly displays both measured and enhanced the prestige of the Ottoman rulers.

The decoration on the backrest of the throne of Ahmed I (right) is of mother-of-pearl, tortoise shell, and precious stones. Suleiman I wore an emerald and ruby brooch (below) in his turban. An example of a simpler style is Bayezid I's wrought-iron lamp (below right).

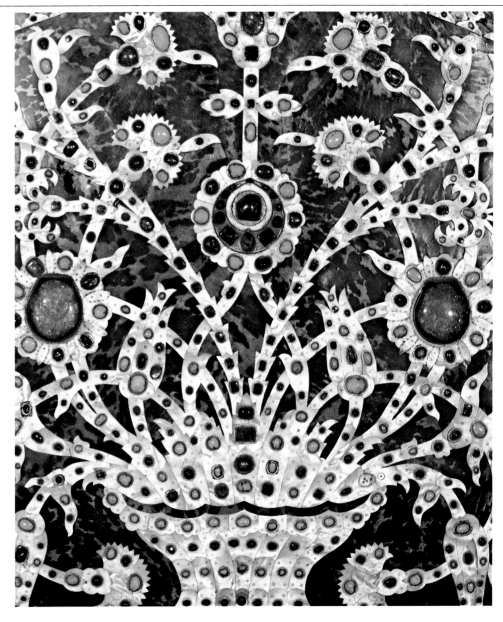

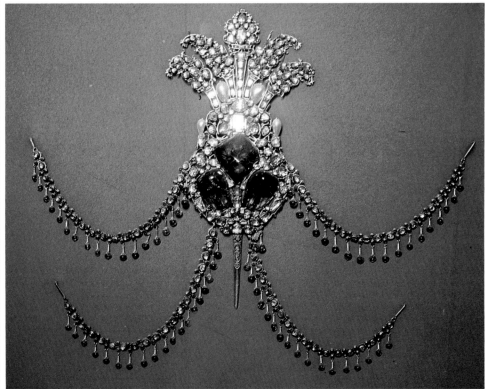

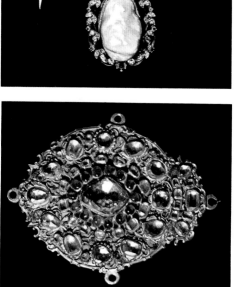

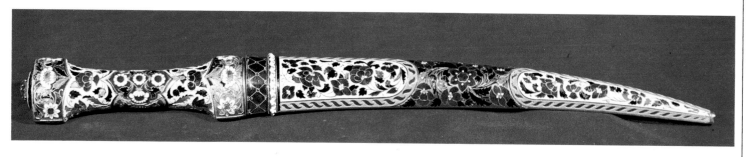

The treasures on this page demonstrate the Persian influence on Ottoman art. Top right, a detail of the back of the throne presented to Mahmud I by the shah of Persia in 1747. This delicate inlay of pearls and precious stones was actually done in Persia, but the elaborate earring (top left), the jeweled night lamp (center left), the gold and emerald dagger (immediately above), and the book-binding of gold enamel and jewels (right) are all Ottoman products clearly resembling Persian work. The blade of the dagger, not seen here, is inlaid with gold and silver thread.

Great of Russia recaptured Azov from the Turks. In 1699, in the Treaty of Karlowitz, the Ottomans gave up all claim to Transylvania, Podolia, the Ukraine, the Peloponnesus, and Dalmatia.

The Ottoman Empire now faced its two ultimate enemies, Austria and Russia. During the eighteenth century, the Austrians were engaged in other European wars, and after their frontier with the Turks had

been stabilized along the Danube they were satisfied, at least for a while. But the czars of Russia were determined to make Russia a major power, and hence sought ports on the Black Sea and access through the Bosporus and the Dardanelles to the Mediterranean. They also wanted Istanbul, which they already called Tzargrad.

The Turks went to war three times during the eighteenth century to maintain their screen of Tatar vassals between Russia and the Black Sea, and twice they were successful. But a third war, beginning in 1768, was disastrous to them. The Russian armies of Catherine the Great defeated the Turks in the Crimea and Ukraine and penetrated as far as the Danube. A Russian fleet from the Baltic sailed around Europe to

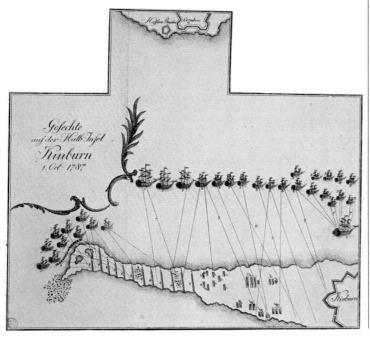

Above, Venetian fleet entering the roadstead of Tripoli during the latter part of the eighteenth century. Left, schematic drawing of an unsuccessful Ottoman attempt to take the fortress of Kinburn, in the Ukraine, during the Russo-Turkish war of 1787. Right, Mohammed Ali Pasha, the Ottoman governor of Egypt in the early nineteenth century. He organized his own army and navy along European lines and soon was challenging the authority of the sultans, who were forced to ask his aid against the Greek uprising.

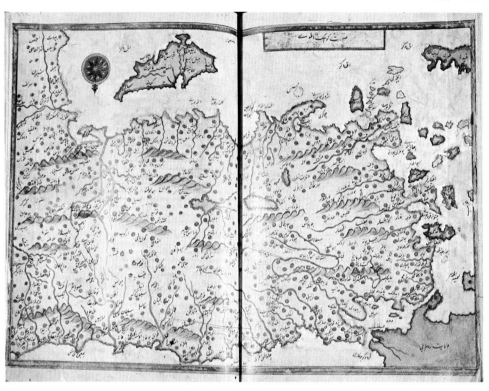

Above, an eighteenth-century Turkish map of Asia Minor. The region is shown inverted because Islamic Orthodoxy insisted that Mecca, the holy city, always be shown at the top, above everything else. Otherwise the map is remarkably accurate.

the Aegean Sea, incited revolts among the Greeks, and destroyed a Turkish fleet off the coast of Asia Minor. In a series of agreements beginning with the humiliating Treaty of Kuchuk Kaynarji in 1774, the Turks gave up the Crimea and the Ukraine to Russia, the czar was recognized as *padishah,* or emperor, and the Russians won the right to navigate through the straits and trade in Ottoman ports. The treaties also allowed Russia to build an Orthodox church in Istanbul and to send representatives to the Porte on behalf of the Orthodox community; this was the beginning of a later Russian claim to the right of protection for all Orthodox Christians within the Ottoman Empire.

The Turks were slow to realize that they were being left far behind by the political, economic, and technical progress of the West. During a period of peace and luxury early in the eighteenth century, they were briefly involved with Western culture, albeit superficially. Tulips imported from Holland became a fashion in the court of Sultan Ahmed III, and for years artists concentrated on the flower as a decorative theme. A Turkish envoy to Paris learned French, reported enthusiastically on French customs and sciences, and came back with a printing press on which he was permitted to publish secular works. Some new Western military techniques were introduced but no

attempt was made to compete with Western factories, which were selling the Turks finished textile, metal, and food products in exchange for raw materials. Although the trade balance was tipping against the Turks, the conservative ulema, who dominated the intellectual climate of Istanbul, were opposed to the idea of westernization, insisting that nothing could be learned from unenlightened infidels who had been repeatedly conquered by Islam.

Not until the defeats at the hands of Russia did the Turks begin any drastic reforms. Sultan Selim III came to the throne in 1789 and proclaimed a "New Order." He brought in French instructors to reorga-

nize and train an infantry force based on the European model, created military and naval schools, and established permanent Turkish embassies in London, Berlin, Vienna, and Paris for the first time. Selim III also promulgated new tax regulations and imposed stronger central control over the janissaries. Conservative resistance to these changes, from the ulema, provincial officials, and janissaries (who rightly feared that the new army would be their downfall), eventually forced Selim III to surrender the throne in 1807, and his successor abolished the reforms. But enough Turks had been exposed to modern ideas to support future moves toward westernization.

To the West, however, the weakness of the Ottoman state was obvious. No longer a threat after their defeat in Vienna in 1683, the Turks and their customs and costumes became quaint curiosities. A *turquerie* style of decoration in France mirrored Istanbul's Tulip Era, and by 1782 the Viennese—who had opened their first coffee house after capturing a store of Turkish coffee outside their gates—could laugh at the Turkish influences in Mozart's "Abduction from the Seraglio." But Ottoman weakness was far from a frivolous concern to the statesmen of Europe, particularly those of Britain and France. For if the Ottoman state were to fall to Russia or Austria (and those two powers had already once plotted to carve it up between them), the victor would control the vital straits and the entire Levant and thereby become a predominant power. This was the essence of the "Eastern Question" that worried the diplomats of

To regain control of Greece after the 1821 revolt, the sultan called in Ali Pasha's Egyptian forces. A Greek hero in the conflict was Andreas Miaulis (top left), a naval commander. Above right, the acropolis of Corinth, one of the last Greek cities retaken by the Turks and Egyptians. In 1927, the European powers stepped in and defeated the Egyptians in the battle of Navarino (left), depicted in a painting by Boutewerk. In 1832, the powers forced the Porte to accept the independence of Greece and its new king, Prince Otto of Bavaria (right), here entering Nauplia in the Peloponnesus.

The Byzantine church of Hagia Sophia became a mosque in 1453. Minarets were added (below right), crosses and Christian symbols were obliterated (below) or plastered over, and a mosaic of Christ on the cupola was covered with Arabic calligraphy (right). The hexagonal pavilion in the interior (facing page) is the sultan's seat. The building is now a museum and many Byzantine mosaics have been restored to view.

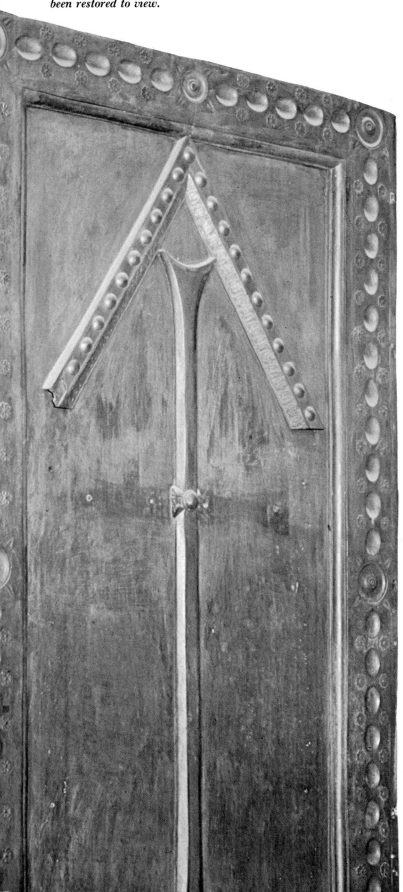

Europe for more than a century: how to support the Turkish Empire against big power ambitions and nationalist revolts so that it could continue to serve as a harmless buffer. The Ottomans, who had entered Europe by playing power politics with European pawns, thus became a pawn in the European game, and their long-time enemy, the Holy Alliance of western European nations, was committed to preserving their territorial boundaries.

For decades, the Russians had encouraged the Greeks to rise against their Turkish masters, and in 1821 the Greeks finally did so. Unable to put down the revolt, the Turks called on their governor of Egypt, Mohammed Ali Pasha, who commanded a modern, efficient, semiautonomous army and navy of his own. By 1827, the Egyptian forces had succeeded in reestablishing Ottoman control over Greece. But by that time pro-Greek liberal volunteers such as Lord Byron, who died in Greece, had roused their homelands, and the Western powers took up the Greek cause. A combined British-French-Russian fleet defeated the Egyptian-Turkish navy off Navarino late in 1827, and, following further Turkish losses to Russian armies, the Greeks gained their independence in 1830.

Facing page, photographs of the Crimean War, taken by Roger Fenton and developed in his van (top left). Top right, interior of a Russian battery. Center right, a mortar battery. Below right, the Valley of Balaclava, scene of the Charge of the Light Brigade. Above, a painting showing the fighting around Sebastopol.

Greece was only one of several chunks that broke off from the Ottoman Empire at about the same time. New Russian invasions took away Bessarabia; Serbian independence had to be recognized; the Romanian provinces of Moldavia and Wallachia achieved greater autonomy; and, in 1830, the French occupied Algeria. The following year, Ali Pasha of Egypt seized his opportunity. With the support of France, he gained control of Syria and, aware that he was more powerful than his sultan, sent his troops deep into Anatolia. Practically defenseless because of internal turmoil, Sultan Mahmud II turned in desperation to his greatest foreign enemy, Russia.

It was a fateful move, another turning point in the fall of the Ottoman Empire. In agreeing to send troops to the Asian shore of the Bosporus to protect Istanbul from its own Egyptian army, Czar Nicholas demanded and received from the sultan the exclusive right to send warships through the straits as well as the pledge that the Ottomans would consult with Moscow on all matters affecting "tranquility and safety." The Russian presence persuaded Ali Pasha to

agree to a compromise peace, and Istanbul was saved. Egypt, however, had become independent in all but name and the Ottoman Empire itself was under Russia's will.

Mahmud II, who came to the throne in 1808, was anxious to resume the westernization program of Selim III. He was forced to act slowly at first, but the Greek rebellion and the other military disasters made it clear even to some conservatives that internal reform was imperative. During a lull in the Greek war, he organized another new, modern army corps, this one trained by Prussian officers and outfitted in Western-style uniforms. The janissaries, naturally, rebelled—for the last time. On June 15, 1826, they

The first war photographer

The Crimean War was the first great conflict to be documented by photographs. The photographer was Roger Fenton, an Englishman, who traveled around the scenes of action in a horse-drawn van containing his darkroom. He could not take any action shots for he had to expose his plates for at least twenty seconds. His plates had to be coated with a moist collodion solution immediately before exposure, and they had to be developed before the solution dried. That meant that he could not be more than a minute or two away from his van when he took his pictures.

Anatolian dwellings

The Turks of Anatolia developed a style of residential architecture that reflected their heritage, their society, and the land itself. Houses were usually built around a central courtyard, recalling the caravansaries or the circle of tents protecting the ancestral nomads' flocks and horses. Within, there was usually little furniture, all of it very low; this too reflected the lifestyle of the nomads, who could carry little with them. The intricate carved and painted designs on the inner walls and ceilings probably developed from the carpets and rich cloths that hung in the ancient tents of the wealthy, but the emphasis on indoor rather than outdoor decoration may also have been simple prudence, for ostentatious displays would attract the tax collector. The façades of Moslem homes were generally painted in brilliant reds, yellows, and blues; non-Moslems could use only browns and grays. Upper stories rested on wooden pillars and lintels, not on the outdoor walls of stone or masonry. This provided protection from earthquakes: The rigid walls might crack and tumble but the wooden frame itself could absorb the shocks.

Right, a well-preserved mansion near Amasya, southern Anatolia. The large, airy galleries gave the residents a fine view of terraced gardens. The skill of the eighteenth-century Turkish architects and carpenters is evident in three interior views below: a semidomed vault containing a calligraphic escutcheon (left), a decorated ceiling presenting a woven effect (center), and a fireplace in a private chamber (right).

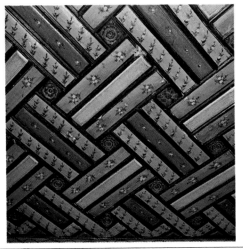

The projecting upper stories (above right) of Anatolian houses increased living space without encroaching on the narrow streets of the towns; a fully laden cart could pass beneath. The broad eaves shielded the interior from the summer sun but allowed the rays of the lower winter sun to penetrate. Right, a reception room in the mansion of an Ottoman official. The painting of Istanbul on the wall above the doors is a typical example of the lively popular art of the eighteenth century.

Western artists delighted in depicting the strange costumes of the Turks. The figures (above, left to right) are said to be two officials, an officer, and a sailor, and the belligerent fellow below is a nineteenth-century depiction of a janissary.

stormed toward the palace along their habitual path of revolt, where Mahmud, with loyal troops and massed artillery, was waiting. Thousands were slaughtered, and later the same day, Mahmud II declared the janissary corps disbanded and ordered that janissary garrisons in the provinces be killed.

Having eliminated the conservatives' power base, the sultan abolished the slave-administrator system and created a new bureaucracy of better-paid officials, who were theoretically less susceptible to bribes. He set up a new school to train them in secular subjects that the religious colleges would not teach and required the new civil servants to wear Western clothes and a new hat, the fez, instead of the traditional turban. His most significant innovation was the translation bureau, which handled the increased diplomatic correspondence, trained young Turks in European languages, and produced many high officials of the government. Finally, to keep all his officials informed, Mahmud II started the first Turkish newspaper and inaugurated a postal system.

Despite their seemingly broad range, the reforms of Mahmud II were superficial, concerned more with form than substance. But almost immediately after his death in 1839, the Porte issued a reform that struck at the Islamic foundations of the state. Known as the Noble Rescript of the Rose Chamber, the new decree was primarily the work of the Ottoman foreign minister, Mustafa Reshid Pasha. Although established in large part to foster internal regeneration and strength, it was also a response to the precarious diplomatic and political situation in which the Turks found themselves. The Ottoman state existed on the sufferance of the big powers. If the Ottomans wanted Western support—against Ali Pasha, who had established an efficient westernized government in Egypt and was once again threatening Istanbul, and of course against the ever-present Russian threat—it would be advantageous to show Turkey's willingness to become a liberal, modern nation in line with Western views and practices.

The Rescript of the Rose Chamber, first in a series

Above left, a Western illustration of the launching of a new ship in Istanbul's Taskizak shipyards in about 1880. A sultan's reception of a foreign ambassador (top) was marked by protocol often mysterious to the Westerner. Immediately above, a deputy grand vizier (left) and the chief gatekeeper of the sultan's palace (right), taken from a work published in 1831.

of reforms known collectively as the *Tanzimat,* or Reorganization, went far toward establishing Western ideas. Besides proclaiming such principles as fair, public trials and the security of life and property, the rescript declared that all Ottoman citizens enjoyed equal protection under the law—regardless of race or religion. This provision pleased the Christian nations, and they immediately converged to work out a compromise between Ali Pasha and the Porte. But the provision violated the fundamental Islamic concept that infidels, though tolerated and allowed a degree of autonomy, were clearly separate and inferior. To treat Christians in the same manner as Moslems went

Abdul-Hamid II (above) was the last sultan to rule personally. His long reign began auspiciously with the promulgation of a constitution in 1876, but he dissolved parliament after a disastrous war with Russia. The conflict was the culmination of a Russian effort to incite all the Slavic peoples of the Balkans to rise against the Turks.

Contemporary prints on these pages depict the Russo-Turkish war of 1877. After marching through Rumania, Czar Alexander and his armies crossed the Danube (above left) on June 24 and advanced through Bulgaria, while another Russian army invaded Turkish territory east of the Black Sea and penetrated Armenia (center left). At Plevna, the czar's Bulgarian advance was checked for five months by a determined force of Turks (left). The Turks' desperate hand-to-hand fighting at Plevna won them new sympathy abroad. Nevertheless, the Russians reached the Sea of Marmara and the Turks signed a humiliating peace at San Stefano in 1878. Right, a fanciful Western view of Turkish artillery.

against the deepest beliefs of the ulema, who were also upset by the rescript's promise of new laws. According to the ulema, the only law was the Koran.

Although the conservatives sabotaged many of the Tanzimat reforms, the decrees continued, covering law, education, finance, military conscription, and provincial administration. Power swung back and forth between Reshid Pasha, who held the post of grand vizier several times, and the conservative ulema, with the young sultan Abdul-Mejid I caught between them. In 1852, the ulema forced Reshid out of office because of a new commercial code he had promulgated two years earlier and his attempt to set up a judiciary independent of the Moslem courts, which had always dispensed Ottoman justice. But he returned in 1854 to see his policies rewarded by European aid in the Crimean War. Impressed by the reforms, Britain and France joined the Ottomans in repelling the Russian attempt to protect the Orthodox Christians in Turkey. The Treaty of Paris of 1856 guaranteed the Turks freedom from Russian interference and technically restored the Turks to the status of a great power. This would not have been possible without the Tanzimat.

The Tanzimat spirit encouraged the Western idea of individualism, which went hand in hand with a vogue for translations of Western novels and poetry and for Western-style journalism. Riding the crest of this current was a group of intellectuals, the New Ottomans. Infused with Western ideals, yet proud of their own Islamic heritage, they began to develop a patriotism based neither on loyalty to the sultan nor on a Turkish identity. Instead, their devotion was based on their love for the Ottoman Empire itself. These somewhat conflicting beliefs led them to oppose the bureaucracy because of its disregard for Islam and because of the special privileges it had extended to foreigners under the system of "capitulations."

The solution, as the New Ottomans saw it, lay in some form of representative assembly that could serve as a restraint on the bureaucracy while at the same time bringing about Islamic democracy. In 1876, the New Ottomans and a small group of officials who shared their aims drafted a constitution for the empire and induced a new sultan, Abdul-Hamid II, to proclaim it. It was a moderately liberal document which left ultimate control in the sultan's hands. Elections were held—the first ever in a Moslem country—and the assembly convened the following

year. But when the debates made clear that all seg-ments of the empire wanted further radical reform and when the deputies asked that certain ministers of the government be brought before them to answer charges, Sultan Abdul-Hamid angrily dissolved the chamber and sent the delegates home. The parlia-ment was not to meet again for thirty years. Thus ended the era of the Tanzimat reforms.

Adding to the sultan's ire was the fact that he was simultaneously losing another war to the Russians. The conflict was ostensibly started to punish the Turks for atrocities they had committed against a Bulgarian uprising, which itself had been instigated by the Russians as part of their Pan-Slavic campaign against the Turks. In this war, neither the British nor the French came to Turkey's aid. Despite the new Turkish army's brilliant defense of the town of Plevna, which blocked the Russians for five months

and earned the Turks new respect in the West, Rus-sian troops marched through Adrianople to the out-skirts of Istanbul while another Russian army at-tacked through the Caucasus and grabbed parts of eastern Anatolia. Terms of peace were settled at the Congress of Berlin in 1878: Siberia, Romania, and Montenegro gained complete independence from the Turks, as did a portion of Bulgaria; Bosnia-Hercego-vina was handed to Austria; and the Turks had to give the Russians part of Transcaucasia. For their part in mitigating Russia's original demands and for promising to defend Turkey from the Russians next time, the French were awarded Tunis and the British were given Cyprus.

This military-diplomatic disaster made Abdul-Hamid II suspicious of the European powers. Al-though he invited the Europeans, particularly the Germans, to build new railway lines, telegraph sys-

At the Congress of Berlin in 1878 (above), the European powers restored to Turkey some of the territories given up in the Treaty of San Stefano, but the Turks still lost most of their Balkan possessions. Sultan Abdul-Hamid's rule became increasingly dictatorial, leading eventually to the Young Turks revolt of 1908, depicted (above right) as a symbolic Turkey exhorting the people. The sultan was forced to reconvene parliament after a thirty-year lapse. After an abortive counterrevolt, parliament voted unanimously to depose him, and a delegation was sent to break the news to him (right) and consign him to exile.

Greeks versus Turks

The historical enmity between Greek and Turk erupted into outright war again in 1896. This time the main issue was the island of Crete. The Turks had ruled the island for two centuries, but most of the people there were Greek-speaking Christians, and after Greece became independent, they grew increasingly restive under the oppressive Ottoman control, particularly during Sultan Abdul-Hamid's reign. When a major revolt flared in 1896, the Turks sent reinforcements to their garrisons and this time Greece responded with naval and land forces. As the fighting escalated, the European powers intervened and sent in an international peace-keeping force, but the powers themselves were divided, with Russia and Germany demanding the Greeks withdraw while England, France, and Italy wanted the Turks to cede autonomy to Crete. In 1897, the war spread to the mainland. The Sultan's troops defeated the Greeks on the frontiers of Macedonia and Thessaly and advanced towards Athens. Again the powers intervened. Eventually the Greek dynasty was saved but Greece paid an indemnity to Istanbul. The Turks also had to give up Crete. Prince George of Greece became governor of the island, which remained under nominal Turkish suzerainty for a time, but all Turkish forces had to withdraw in 1898, leaving actual control in the hands of the big powers.

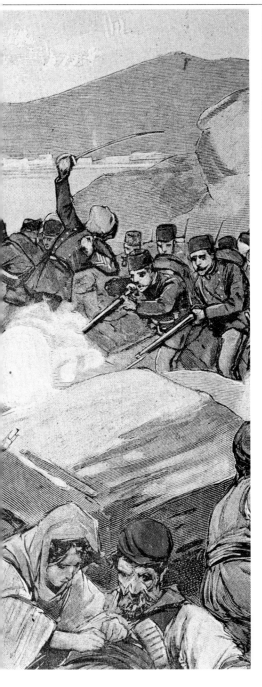

Scenes of the Greco-Turkish War of 1896–97: Far left, fighting at Canea, the ancient capital of Crete. Above, Greeks on the barricades of Macedonia, on the mainland. Turkish cavalry charges were decisive in defeating the Greeks in Thessaly (left). The European powers, whose trade was hurt by the conflict, occupied key points in Crete with an international force (top right) and bombarded the coast of Crete (center right) in an effort to end the war. Right, Greek and Turkish officers discussing the terms of the cease-fire. Even after the war was formally over, the island of Crete remained in turmoil under international control. Far right, Russian soldiers in a clash with local inhabitants.

Mohammed V (left), Turkey's next-to-last sultan, presided over the dismemberment of the empire. After losing the Balkan War in 1913, Turkey was forced into an armistice (below) with Bulgaria, which cost it most of its Balkan lands. Entering World War I on the losing side finally doomed the dynasty. The new Republic of Turkey, symbolized in posters as an unveiled woman (right) leading Mustafa Kemal's horse, moved the capital to Ankara (below left) in 1922.

Mohammed V (left), Turkey's next-to-last sultan, presided over the dismemberment of the empire. After losing the Balkan War in 1913, Turkey was forced into an armistice (below) with Bulgaria, which cost it most of its Balkan lands. Entering World War I on the losing side finally doomed the dynasty. The new Republic of Turkey, symbolized in posters as an unveiled woman (right) leading Mustafa Kemal's horse, moved the capital to Ankara (below left) in 1922.

tems, mines, and public utilities, he became increasingly anti-Western. To court popularity, he promoted Islamic solidarity, but he trusted neither Moslem nor Christian and turned the empire into a police state laced with spies and censors. In the 1890s, a number of non-Turkish ethnic groups within the empire began to agitate for autonomy, and when the Armenian revolutionary groups rose in revolt, the sultan suppressed them with great massacres; he was soon being called "Abdul the Damned" in the West.

Abdul-Hamid's reign grew so repressive that a number of educated Turks from the military and medical schools began plotting against him in a secret organization called the Committee of Union and Progress (CUP). When a CUP plot to overthrow the regime was exposed, many of its leaders were exiled or fled abroad, giving them the opportunity to publish opposition newspapers and smuggle them into the country. As the clandestine opposition to the sultan spread, the emergent party took up the name "Turk," a designation that the Ottoman elite had previously used to refer to ignorant peasants. The CUP came to be known as the "Young Turks," and branches sprang up all over the empire.

This ferment came to a head in 1908 in Salonika, the headquarters of the Ottoman Third Army. The CUP organization there included many army officers incensed at the sultan for having allowed troops from the great powers to enter that city to combat Bulgarian guerrillas. On July 21, 1908, after the assassination of a general sent to quell mutinies in Salonika, the CUP there telegraphed the sultan demanding that he restore the long-suspended constitution and call elections. Accepting the inevitable, the sultan complied. Amidst great popular enthusiasm the exiles returned and a new parliament, composed mostly of men supported by the CUP, was elected.

In his speech to the opening session, Sultan Abdul-Hamid gave the impression that he would perform as

İSTİKLÂL SAVAŞININ MUZAFFER GARP CEPHESİ KOMUTANI İNÖNÜ LOZANDAN ANAYURDA SULH ve ZAFER GETİRİYOR.

GELDİK SANA BAYRAMLARLA EY GÜZEL ÜLKE

AY YILDIZI SAR KOYNUNDA GÜZEL SEV BESLE

a constitutional monarch. But a few months later, with his support, army troops launched a coup d'état against the CUP government; the parliament chamber was invaded and some CUP officials were massacred. When Third Army troops descended on the capital—by train—and restored the chamber, the deputies voted to depose the sultan. In accordance with the Koran, the Sheikh-ul-Islam (the highest religious authority) was consulted, and he agreed. Three decades earlier, Abdul-Hamid had dismissed parliament; in 1909 it dismissed him. Unlike some of his ancestors, he was only exiled, not strangled.

With the beginning of constitutional government, under the figurehead reign of Sultan Mohammed V, Turkey entered a period of feverish domestic politicking and witnessed further external defeats. The CUP, favoring tight central control over a "Turkified" empire, was generally in control but found itself challenged by the Liberal Union—deputies who urged a more relaxed central authority. But the CUP members were themselves divided and the issues were not sharply defined. External events soon rendered academic these debates about whether the empire should be essentially "Turkish" or "Ottoman."

In 1911, Italy invaded Tripoli (modern Libya) and bombarded Rhodes and other Ottoman islands. The Turkish navy had declined in strength under Abdul-Hamid, and the Istanbul government was forced to give up its last territory in Africa. That defeat was followed by the Balkan War of 1912, in which a coalition of Greece, Serbia, and Bulgaria, in a series of coordinated attacks from three directions, forced the Turks to retreat completely across the Balkan peninsula, from Albania, through Macedonia and Thrace, until they held only a small strip of territory around Istanbul. In a second Balkan War a few months later, while the three victors fought among themselves, the Turks regained Adrianople and eastern Thrace. The net result was nevertheless an Ottoman catastrophe, for it reduced Turkey's European possessions to approximately the region Murad I had conquered in the fourteenth century. These defeats turned the Young Turks into a military dictatorship that did not hesitate to fix elections or assassinate opponents to gain its ends.

The Young Turks had rebelled to save the empire, but in the end they were responsible for its fall. On August 2, 1914, the day after Germany declared war against Russia, Ottoman War Minister Enver Pasha signed an alliance with Germany. For three months the treaty was kept secret, not only from the world and the Turkish people but from most of the members of the government, for most Turks would have preferred to remain neutral in the Great War. But Enver, one of the army-officer heroes of the 1908 revolution, was certain that Germany would defeat the Turks' old enemy—Russia—and he wanted to be involved in the victory.

Enver's miscalculation cost the Turks everything. They were forced to fight on a number of scattered fronts just to protect their own territory. Although they contributed substantial force to Germany's war effort, only at Gallipoli, where Turkish troops beat back a huge British-French attempt to open a sea route to Russia through the Dardanelles, could the Ottomans claim a significant victory.

When the war ended in defeat for the Central Powers, Enver Pasha and other CUP leaders slipped away to Germany. The British occupied Istanbul and forced Sultan Mohammed VI to sign the Treaty of Sèvres, which ceded Thrace and part of the Anatolian coast to Greece, recognized Arab and Armenian autonomy, granted the Allies control over Istanbul and the straits, and generally destroyed the independence of Turkey. With this humiliating surrender forced on the last, helpless descendant of the House of Osman, the Ottoman Empire came to an end. For two more years, the puppet sultan continued to occupy his throne and palace. But during that time, a new nationalist movement under the leadership of Mustafa Kemal, known as "Ataturk," established a republic that drove the Greeks out of Asia Minor and restored a measure of dignity to the Turkish people. In 1922, the assembly of the new Republic of Turkey formally declared that the sultanate no longer existed. In recognition of Ataturk's remarkable qualities of leadership and to thank him for his victory over the Greeks, the new assembly reached back into its heritage and bestowed on the modern leader the ancient and honorable title of "Ghazi."

Photography Credits

Index